HUN

MW00526907

"When Jeff Brown dares to speak truth about our spiritual lives, the curtain that's been covering the wizard comes tumbling down and we recognize that it's just a dude with his fingers on the controls of our souls and we are emboldened to take back our sovereignty and lament and praise with the whole of our authentic broken open hearts. This little book is a loose thread. Pull it."

—MIRABAI STARR, author of *Caravan of No Despair*
and *Wild Mercy*

"Jeff Brown is an abiding voice throughout time. His words not only speak to us right now, but also look back to instill clarity to the bewildering sources, causes, and places of where we were, fathering our steps with his special brand of strong courage as we venture into an ever-changing world. Jeff's newest work, *Humanifestations,* blankets every human theme imaginable with warm wisdom. Our traumatic experiences, our relationship to emerging truths, and our ongoing transformation are held in caring eyes. Read and be nourished by every affirming morsel. You will feel emboldened by each page. You will come to understand and appreciate the sanctity of your purpose. And you'll want to keep this potent, validating book with you as you trek into tomorrow."

—SUSAN FRYBORT, author of *Open Passages* and
Look to The Clearing

"Everything Jeff Brown writes has a unique salty feisty savor. He is one of our truly magnificent rebels of the heart. Always looking for new ways to wake us up to the ragged glory of our embodiment and relentlessly both funny and scathing about our inabilities to be simply human. I love *Humanifestations* and recommend it to all those who know the divine lives in us and as us."

—ANDREW HARVEY, co-author of *Radical Regeneration*
with Carolyn Baker

"Jeff's writing cuts through the gauzy veils of mainstream spirituality. He's an iconoclast by nature, overturning new age tropes with refreshing honesty, but never at the expense of tenderness."

—TOKO-PA TURNER, bestselling author of *Belonging:*
Remembering Ourselves Home

"I've always found Jeff Brown's words to be honest, brave, timely, and timeless, and his latest offering is no exception. Comprised of short, pith-like entries, *Humanifestations* encourages (and challenges) readers to take an intimate, unflinching look at ourselves, our paradigms, our hearts, our souls, and what it means to be a truly present, transparent and embodied human. In other words, *Humanifestations* is yet another mic drop moment for Jeff Brown. 100%."

—CHRIS GROSSO, author of *Indie Spiritualist* and
Necessary Death

"Jeff Brown celebrates... no, stands for, advocates for, fiercely forwards our humanity. That means our traumas and sufferings, our need for compassion and fury, our light and shadow. This book offers daily doses of medicine – medicine that embraces the WHOLE of us, medicine that says "YES" to our messy muddy selves, medicine that serves to activate our immune systems against the seductions of a bypass, and naive "let it go," "just forgive" culture. Brown offers a vision of a world where we all belong, a world that I truly feel I can live in."

—DAVID BEDRICK, author of *You Can't Judge a Body by its Cover*

"In yet another masterful piece of work, Jeff Brown's *Humanifestations* speaks to the depths of the human condition and offers us helpful, realistic and compassionate insights and advice. His perspective honors our biopsychosocial and spiritual make-up and is true to the most recent research and recommendations for trauma recovery. The vast landscape of healing and spirituality is inundated with misguided platitudes that often steer us away from where we should be going. Jeff's refreshingly honest and exacting quotes are a beacon to follow."

—CARMEN CASADO, Integrative Somatic Therapist

"Jeff Brown is a master at comprehending what actualization entails. His offering in this book encourages us to move toward, not away from, our humanity. He understands that we find true freedom through the wisdom of the body. Jeff invites us to stop and listen to the wisdom of our souls, urging us to take a step closer towards our own self-actualization. His cry for us to hear the call of our soul is life giving. He suggests that our ability to connect with others increases as we become more authentically connected to ourselves. Oh the joy of that! *Humanifestations* is a beautiful rallying call to live and love in authenticity. it is both an honouring of the human condition and an inspiration for the spirit. Simply beautiful."

—SHAUNA QUIGLEY, creator of the 'Clearing Method'

Other Books by Jeff Brown

Soulshaping: A Journey of Self-Creation
Ascending with Both Feet on the Ground
Love It Forward
An Uncommon Bond
Spiritual Graffiti
Grounded Spirituality
Hearticulations

HUMANIFESTATIONS

On Trauma,
Truth, and
Transformation

Jeff Brown

ENREALMENT PRESS
HAMILTON, ONTARIO

Published by Enrealment Press
PO Box 65618,
Dundas, Ontario, Canada
L9H-6Y6

Cover background image by Grey Carnation/Shutterstock
Cover lined paper image by and lllonajalll/Shutterstock
Illustration on page 178 by Happy Pictures/Shutterstock
Cover design by Susan Frybort
Book design by Allyson Woodrooffe
Printed in the USA

Library and Archives Canada Cataloguing in Publication

Title: Humanifestations : on trauma, truth, and transformation /
    Jeff Brown.
Names: Brown, Jeff, 1962- author.
Identifiers: Canadiana (print) 20230182550 | Canadiana (ebook)
    20230182682 | ISBN 9781988648132 (softcover) | ISBN
    9781988648149 (PDF)
Subjects: LCSH: Brown, Jeff, 1962-—Quotations. | LCSH: Psychic
    trauma—Quotations, maxims, etc. | LCSH: Truth—Quotations,
    maxims, etc. | LCSH: Change—Quotations, maxims, etc. |
    LCSH: Change (Psychology)—Quotations, maxims, etc. |
    LCSH: Interpersonal relations—Quotations, maxims, etc.
Classification: LCC PN6081 .B76 2023 | DDC 158—dc23

*For Lily. The bravest humanifestation
I have ever known.*

HUMANIFESTATIONS

On Trauma,
Truth, and
Transformation

There are two forms of courage in this world. One demands that we jump into action with our armor on.

The other demands that we strip ourselves bare-naked and surrender. Bravery is a curious thing.

Don't "Get over it!" Get inside of it. Get to the heart of it. Get through it. Your painful story is not some hurdle to jump over. It's not a pole to vault. It's a lived experience that longs for your attention. It's a trauma that awaits your compassion. It's an embodied truth that demands to be expressed. So next time someone tells you to "get over it," just say NO. And then tell them to "get over" their need to trivialize other people's challenges. Ask them to look deeply at how this repressive mantra has prevented them from healing their own wounds. They are unlikely to know… but the seed you plant may well yield fruits when the moment is ripe.

You can't reason with the nervous system. It has a mind of its own. But you can listen close when it tells you what it needs to self-regulate. Listen in, and honor its requests to the letter. That's where the healing happens. In the listening.

Practice the art of selective attachment, the process of sifting everything through an essential filter, connecting only to those experiences and relationships that support your true-path. Kind of like a heart with a gate at the opening, it creaks open only when you make the conscious decision to unlatch the gate and welcome in the next lesson on your path. If something supports your growth, bring it on. If it doesn't, stay away.

I have no capacity to engage in conversations that aren't entirely truthful and brave. I love courageous conversations that clarify confusion and heal the rifts. Where everyone makes admissions and owns their mistakes. Cryptic, misleading, politically staged conversations are an insult to everyone's intelligence. And a waste of everyone's time. Real talk, or no talk at all.

The assumptive term "victim mentality" has to go. It's just another way that a repressive culture shames and shuns woundedness. When I grew up it was: "Don't be a cry-baby," and "Leave the past behind you." Yes, it is true that we can become imprisoned inside of our woundedness. But the term "victim mentality" suggests otherwise. It suggests that a choice is being made to remain affixed to our wounds. And how can we know that from the outside? We can't. Someone can certainly make that statement about themselves. But we can't make it about them. Because we aren't walking in their shoes. We aren't inside of their traumatic memories. For all we know, they carry more trauma than we could ever imagine. Perhaps they are the bravest and most hopeful person we have ever encountered. Just to get up every day and believe, is a remarkable victory for many. So be careful when you talk about someone's "victim mentality." You may be talking about someone who has achieved a greater victory than you.

I call it the "narcissism of progress." It's when you grow and evolve, and then project the assumption of growth onto others, as though they are you and see the world through your eyes. It's not a malevolent tendency. It's simply a misplaced (and often hopeful) assumption of transformation. You reach a place where you couldn't act in a certain way, and then assume that someone else is there, too. And sometimes, they are. And sometimes... they aren't. As much as we long to see everyone grow and evolve, it's important to remember that some people won't do a stitch of work in that regard. They are comfortable (or uncomfortable) right where they are, or they will grow when they are ready, or they simply have a different idea of growth. It's important to understand this, so that you live in relational reality, so that you don't put your eggs in the wrong basket, and so that you experience the liberating benefits of meeting people right where they are. It takes tremendous energy to make assumptions about other people's consciousness. Save it for your own journey. You will surely need it to get where you long to go.

You don't retire from a calling. You retire from a job. A calling is indistinguishable from that which breathes you. You do it, until your very last breath.

Getting close to someone demands that we also get close to ourselves. That's the nature of true intimacy. When our heart opens to another, it also opens to ourself. Love excavates everything alive within us—including our unresolved shadow—in an effort to bring all that we are into the light of connection. It wants the whole of us to be present for the experience. It wants the whole of us to heal. Then our experience of intimacy is something more than a reach for the other. It's also a reach for ourselves. Not merely a fleeting adventure between two souls, but a truly transformative journey towards wholeness.

Do you stand in the fire of truth, or do you often choose convenience? Do you honor the call of your soul, or do you allow your personas to shape your path? Do you trust your deepest knowing, or do you default to the opinion of others? Do you believe in your inherent worth, or do you believe the voice of shame?

What will it take before you can fully trust your brilliance?

"Be Here Now!" We can't. We have too much trauma in the way. "The Power of Now!" sounds good, but first we have to deal with the "Power of Then." Worst things, first. It's easy enough to talk about being in the 'now.' But what are we even talking about? 'Now' through the mind? Through the heart? Through the body? What does it even mean to be fully present? Many of the people teaching 'nowness' are head-tripping, meditation-addicted spiritual bypassers. What do they really know about presence? The truth is that we are all trauma survivors, and that includes every spiritual teacher I have ever known. Almost every one of them has confused self-avoidance with enlightenment, blaming the mind for their problems and issues while conveniently sidestepping their wounded hearts. Bottom line—we can't be in the present, because our emotional and physical bodies are tied up in trauma knots. Threads of our consciousness are still back there, locked into the originating wounds. If we want to truly BE HERE NOW, we have to BE THERE, THEN. We have to untie the knots and heal the core wounds. Then, and only 'then,' will we know the true power of NOW.

We don't do ourselves any service when we resist the journey, when we resist the calls of true-path, when we push down the voices of next step, when we refuse to get on our own boat and cross the river of artifice to the more authentic landscape that awaits us. When we ignore our truth-aches, when we turn back from the river edge, we put ourselves at risk. We drown in our own distractions. We suffer for our avoidance. There really is no benefit to walking in someone else's shoes. We have a unique journey encoded in the bones of our being. We are built to take our own steps. We are built to journey. We are journey.

We are all tired. Really, we are. It's a hard road, but it's also a beautiful one. Perhaps we expect too much from ourselves and from others. Perhaps humanity can only make slow progress, like an inchworm. Perhaps we need to celebrate how far we have come. And rest more. And relish the simple pleasures. And look for love everywhere. There is a river near where I live. It meanders slowly, peacefully. It doesn't ask itself why it isn't an ocean, or a raging river, or some other thing. It just surrenders to what it is. Maybe we just need to surrender more to who we are. I think I will lie down tomorrow beside the river. And take a rest. And sweet surrender.

Trauma isn't someone else's story. It's your story, too. It's everyone's story, whether they know it or not. We may have found a way to repress it, but that doesn't mean it's gone. It's still in there, running the individual and collective show. Only when we make the conscious choice to unpack it, will we be free. Our ancestors had no choice but to bury it, but because of the foundation they laid for us, we can choose otherwise. We can choose to heal ourselves and them, together. We are the pioneers of a healing humanity. What a beautiful opportunity. Let's get to work.

You can't solve the problem if you can't own the problem. That's where many of us get stuck, individually and relationally. We can't admit there's an issue, so we remain trapped deep inside of it. The door to transformation opens the moment we acknowledge that something needs to be resolved. Self-admission turns the key.

It's not about getting to the top of the mountain. It's not about accessing your "higher power." It's not about transcendence. It's not about "rising above" the human condition. What it is actually about is getting to the depths of your being. Your truest power. Your feet planted on Mother Earth. Your humanness. Only from here can we know presence. Only from here can we heal and transform our species. There is no time left for dissociation and denial. No time left for self-avoidance that masquerades as awakening. If we don't get 'here' soon, we are not going to make it. It is time for the great arrival. Not from the Pleiadians. Not from the star-people. From the humans. From us. Right here. Right now. We don't need to rise. We need to ground. We need to return to our bodies, and heal this bloodied species. Are you with me?

When they tell you they had a perfect childhood, RUN. When they tell you they have no issues, RUN. Not because you are addicted to suffering, but because you know that you can't grow with someone, if they can't acknowledge their stuff.

What is an opportunity to one person, is a destructive choice for another. Because each soul is different, and has its own unique directionality. For one, worldly success might be everything. For another, a quiet, creative life is paradise. We really need to understand this, before we express opinions about another's path. This is particularly true for young people, who are easily influenced. The only advice you can give them is to excavate their own true path. If they do that, they have found everything there is.

There is an unmistakable relationship between early life abandonment and the hunger to fully merge with another in love relationship. Because the primal need to bond was not met in infancy, it gets projected forward into intimate relationships in the form of a desperate desire for oneness. We see this often in those who are twin-flame obsessed. Unable to identify where they end and the other begins, they are starving for oneness. But a full merger isn't truly possible, because you cannot actually re-create your early-life dynamics. You can't just go back there, and put someone else in mommy or daddy's place. It only works for so long, before you come crashing back to earth, abandonment wound in tow.

It's fine to learn from people, but we have to be careful not to Godjectify them. Nothing will disempower you more on the path than perpetually projecting God-wisdom onto others. Not only because they may disappoint you, but because it's all too easy to get locked into the safety of a seeker role this way. Finders don't spend their lives looking for wisdom in others. They come to realize that they can only find it within. Yes, others know a little something, but when it comes to your own path, only you can know what steps to take. You are the sculptor of your own reality—don't hand your tools to anyone else.

When someone tells you that you are being "too sensitive," what they are usually telling you is that they are "too insensitive." And, more often than not, that same person will insist that their particular sensitivities are always healthy and appropriate. The most common sentence uttered by narcissists is "You're being too sensitive," when they are confronted with their wrongdoing. It's their favorite way to gaslight their victims. Because there is only one victim allowed on Planet Narco. And it's always them. If someone keeps telling you that you are being "too sensitive" when you share your feelings, it's probably time to take your beautiful sensitivity elsewhere.

It's not about what you are here to bring to the world. It's about what you are here to bring to yourself, first and foremost. The actualization of your callings is fundamental to your own transformation. It is the way you bring yourself into wholeness. And from that place, your offerings radiate outward to touch the world-at-large. It's your bridge to humanity. But it always begins in the bones of your being. Many people choose a path because it is the most likely to get them external validation. That's not a calling. A calling exists in and of itself. You may like that it helps others, but that's not why you do it. You do it because it's who you are. And because you won't know peace without it.

There's a fine and meaningful line between triggers that support our healing, and those that merely re-traumatize us.

Healthy relationships are not expectation sets. They are blessings. It's one thing to expect things that are agreed to, but the moment we begin to expect things that have never been agreed to, we walk on dangerous ground. Because we have no right to expect anything that hasn't been explicitly stated. If you want someone to meet your needs, they have to agree to that. If you want someone to be there for you when life gets difficult, they have to agree to that. If you want someone to behave a certain way, they have to agree to that. If they don't, you can decide that they are no longer a blessing that you want in your life. But you can't fault them for not being someone they haven't agreed to. That was your story. Not theirs. Self-created expectations are the bane of healthy relationship, and take us further away from the intimacy we seek. Forget expectations. Better to let everyone decide for themselves how they wish to show up.

As I look back on my life, there is one thing I have consistently despised: abuse of power. Abuse of parental power, abuse of economic power, abuse of spiritual power, abuse of political power. I don't care if it comes from the right, or the left, or the center. Abuse of power is always a crime against humanity. And there is no chance that we will heal the rifts between us, or co-create the inclusive world we long for, until it becomes extinct.

One of the things that helped me the most was rejecting those who rejected me, rather than chasing their approval. Become an expert at this, and your path will come clear. So much energy gets wasted traveling down dead-end roads. Spot them as soon as you can, and make another choice. You don't owe anyone anything that you haven't chosen. Your only responsibility is to become all that you are meant to become.

The 'toughen-uppers' are the most traumatized of all. They are so traumatized that they don't even know they are in pain. So when they tell you to 'toughen up' when you are hurting, pay them no mind. They want you to put away your pain, so they don't have to be reminded of their own.

Sometimes things happen for us, and sometimes they happen to us. It's an important distinction. Because if you keep believing that every painful thing that happened was a gift, you won't learn the lessons you need to protect yourself. And you won't heal all the unresolved pain that you are carrying. You will just continue to shoot yourself in the foot, imagining it a blessing in disguise. It isn't. It's a gunshot wound. And those kinds of happenings, you can do without.

I used to try to punch my way through people's walls. I didn't understand that they were there for a reason and often essential to their survival. I did the same with my own walls. Neither got me anywhere. The walls just got tougher, denser, more resilient. Now I have a different approach. I pray to walls. I honor their wisdom. I stroke them with kindness. I melt them with gentleness. And, if they still insist on standing firm, I leave them be. Walls have a timeline all their own.

It is still amazing to me how tenacious our self-doubt patterns are, and how quickly our positive self-thoughts can evaporate. This is the stage of the collective unconscious, one where many of us are more inclined to hide our light under a bushel of shame than to celebrate our magnificence. What this tells me is that we have lots of work left to do internally, and, just as importantly, that we need to make a point of validating others whenever possible: "I love you … You are fantastic … I appreciate what is unique about you … I am grateful for your presence … You rock." There can never be too much kindness, too much attunement, too much honoring of the other. Love them forward….

There is a wonderful thing that happens when you stop trying to change people's thinking. You suddenly realize how much energy you have left for the things actually within your control: your well-being, your callings, your healing, your growth, your humanifestations. And you eventually come to see that you were wasting precious time focused on changing others. Not only because you can't actually know what way of thinking is right for another person, but because all the time you spent on them, was time not spent on you. You were devoting so much time to pushing them to transform, that you forgot to transform the only person that you can ... you. You want to change someone's way of thinking? Change yours.

It's not all in your head. It's all in your heart. It's all in your feet. It's all in your hips. It's all in your shoulders. It's all in your breath. It's all in your body. Anything unattended to, unresolved, unhealed, and unprocessed lives in your tissues, your cells, your musculature. It may be manifest in your thinking, but it doesn't begin there. The mind does not source itself—the body does. The trick is to not try to shift your thinking from within the mind itself. You can't. You may be able to subdue it there, but you won't be able to resolve it. Because the troubling thoughts are merely a symptom of the deeper issues. They are a reflection of our emotional holdings and constricted musculature. They emanate from the fleshy trauma tunnels that we dug in order to survive this world. Many of us sit in the waiting room of awakening for decades, waiting impatiently for our new birth. Yet it never arrives, because we are looking for it where it isn't—within the mind, itself. Babies aren't born that way. You have to go down into the depths of the body to bring a new birth to life. Down, down, down... into the alchemical chambers of new thought—YOUR MAGNIFICENT BODY. This is where you are born again.

I often hear people say that we must hold a neutral space for our partner's shadow, so that we can help them to heal it. Sounds good, but it's not entirely realistic. Because we are not little Buddhas in relationship with each other. We are not neutral experiencers. If we are in partnership with someone, we are emotionally and energetically engaged. We cannot be neutral, nor can we be entirely detached from their process. We are inside of it, together. If we are to hold the space for their emerging shadow, then we must also hold space for our own emerging shadow. This makes for a messier relational process, but it also makes for a more authentic transformation.

People often say, "You chose your parents," as though that is an absolute fact. It isn't. Because we can't know why someone ended up with the parents they got. It may have been karma, it may have been accident, it may have been the luck of the draw. It may have been a lot of things, but it's not for us to say. It's for them to say. When we try to say it for them, we deny them their own process and perspective. And, in the case of those who had horrifying parents, we add insult to injury. It's already hard enough to move through life carrying the pain. The last thing you need to hear is that you chose it. Maybe you did, or maybe life is far more complicated than that. And, either way, your healing is your salvation. That's the only choice that matters. And that's the only way to break the ancestral cycle of abuse.

If they tell you that they're awake, they are fast asleep. If they tell you they are "enlightened masters," they are masters of self-avoidance. If they tell you they have "transcended ego," they are ruled by it. If they tell you they have "arrived," they are merely on the way. That's the thing about awakening. It is never a completed journey. There is no king (or queen) of consciousness. We are all a work-in-process. We are all path travelers on a quest for meaning. As you deepen and expand, you quickly 'realeyes' that there is no fixed or absolute state. There is only a relative and fluid state, an ever-expanding foray into the great within and beyond. There is no permanent irrevocable moment of Enlightenment. It is more like spirals of awakening that transmute into a kaleidoscope of richer color and texture, as we evolve into greater spectrums of consciousness, each more complex, nuanced, and intricate than the ones before. Through this lens, you see how far you have come, and you recognize how far you have yet to travel. So many as yet underdeveloped parts, so many ways to touch the moment, so many realms of delicious possibility. There is always more to discover.

If you reached the stage where you have grown beyond your family-of-origin, it's important not to pressure yourself to bring them along with you. You don't have that obligation, and you also don't have that right. In the same way as you didn't want them to define you, they don't want you to define them. It's up to them, just like it was up to you. You may feel sure that you found a more conscious way of being, but they may not agree. And even if they do, it's for them to decide if they want to join you. The world I want to live in is one where everyone gets to pick the path that is true for them. None better than the other. None more worthy of praise. Each of us a pioneer of our own unique path.

I once overheard someone say: "The fact that you don't have money shouldn't stand in the way of your healing. Just do it." I was shocked. In the heart of the challenge of meeting our basic needs, it is all most of humanity can do to endure and survive until things improve. Quite apart from the obvious fact that those living under economic duress cannot afford some of the healing services they need, their consciousness is often so overwhelmed with survivalist anxiety that the last thing they are thinking about is transformation. Food on the table trumps those considerations. For many of us, healing services are an unaffordable luxury. May we not forget that, and may we not shame those who are simply trying to stay alive from moment to moment. Rather than shame them, let us lift them up with emotional and economic support. You want to invite the healing of humanity? Give wherever possible.

Words. So powerful. They can crush a heart, or heal it. They can shame a soul, or liberate it. They can shatter dreams, or energize them. They can obstruct connection, or invite it. They can create defenses, or melt them. We have to use words wisely.

I often hear people talk about how grateful they are that they were traumatized. They claim to have gone through a long healing journey, and to have come out the other side grateful for their realizations and lessons. It is not for me to say that this isn't true— sometimes we do awaken and evolve as a result of our traumas—but what I find interesting, is that it is often the same people who judge those who haven't arrived at a place of gratitude. They look down on them, often suggesting that they are too weak or too attached to their victimhood to do the real work. And it's the 'looking down' that leads me to wonder if they have healed at all. Because if someone has truly converted their trauma into gratitude, then they will be equally aware of the fact that some people cannot. The measure of our healing is not reaching a place where we give thanks for our suffering. It is reaching a place of deep compassion for the traumatized human condition. And understanding that what you went through, was unique to you. It doesn't give you license to judge another. Their wounds, their path.

There is a big difference between projections and hard-earned wisdom. All too often, people are accused of projecting when they make bold statements about human behavior. And sometimes this is true—our perspective can emanate from our own unresolved issues. We still have a chip on our shoulder, and that chip influences our view. But sometimes, our perspective is a reflection of what we have gleaned from our experiences. Sometimes we have learned a little something from all we have endured. So let's not turn everyone's wisdom into a mirror projection game. Because sometimes we are actually seeing through the veils to a truth that demands expression. Sometimes our insights are fully grounded in reality. Sometimes we are seeing things exactly as they are.

Celebrity culture is a huge reason why humanity is locked into a self-diminishing reality. It must be dismantled. Until it is, much of humanity will be living vicariously through a small number of optics-manipulated symbologies, looking up to people they don't even know, making voting decisions based on what their favorite star instructs, wasting precious time that could be spent actualizing their own sacred purpose. With our necks craned to look up to a bunch of fame-seekers, we cannot look down at ourselves to notice the wonder that we are. I appreciate that some celebrities actually have a real talent for something, but so do all of us, if we can only humanifest it. And just because someone has a talent, doesn't mean they know a thing about anything else, nor does it qualify them to take on a bigger role in your life than you do. We are all luminous stars at heart, and it's been my experience that those who actualize their greatness, want nothing to do with public star-dumb. They are too busy bringing their gifts into form.

If one person is done with the relationship, so are you. You just may not know it yet. So, get up to speed, and save yourself precious time. Because there's no time to waste on the quest for lasting love. No time at all.

The way we break free from dysfunctional family patterns is not by running away from them. It's by walking back in their direction. Not because we want to keep repeating them, but because the only way to shift these patterns is to heal them at their roots. It's okay to run from them for a time, but not for all time. Because the flight from what lives inside of you merely delays your arrival. You may think you are on the way to a new destination, yet the plane keeps circling back to your childhood home. It can't navigate a new flight plan until you return back to where you came from and heal your broken wings. With your wings strengthened, there is nowhere you can't go.

I was often criticized for being indecisive, particularly when confronted with decisions around career and relationship. In the practical, survivalist world I came from, there was no time to waste. Decisions had to be made quickly, positions had to be claimed, even if they weren't true to path. But in the authentic world I longed for, significant decisions had to be made slowly, because it often took years to clarify the soul's journey. Because it took years to distinguish true path from conditioned path. Because it took years to learn the lessons necessary to inform significant directional decisions. What they call a late-bloomer in a survivalist world, I call a grounded-grower in an authentic world. Better to take our time and root our decisions in a deep knowing, than race to a path that is not truly our own.

If you grew up in a family that felt like a prison, you may have issues with engulfment throughout your life. You may feel like you are trapped whenever you make a commitment to a relationship, a job, a place to live. If you haven't done enough work to heal the early life issues, it is very easy to project the expectation of suffering onto anything that you have committed to. It all begins to feel like the same old prison, even if it isn't. Symptoms of unresolved engulfment issues include: a perpetual need to be on the move geographically; a persistent quitting of jobs; a never-ending quest for 'the one'; an addiction to 'seeking' (even after 'finding'); the termination of love relationships when they get too close; and the preferring of fantasy and part-time lovers to vulnerable, authentic intimacy with your partner. Sometimes it is true that you are experiencing these symptoms because you are truly not where you belong. But not always. Sometimes it has nothing to do with true-path at all, but everything to do with the need to heal unresolved early-life material. Once healed, the engulfment projections fall away and you can begin to celebrate the commitments that you have chosen. Not a prison in fact, but a liberating opportunity to heal and transform.

Many of us who embark on a self-creation journey find ourselves stuck between two worlds: the survivalist, armored world we come from, and the authentic, inclusive world we long for. In other words, we find ourselves caught between a rock and a 'heart place.' Getting to the other side is no easy task, but there are three things that can help you to stay the course:

1. Finding a soulpod of supportive individuals who are traversing the same terrain.

2. Learning to distinguish between conscious armoring (armoring only when necessary), and unconscious armoring (armoring as a patterned response) as a way of being.

3. Excavating and actualizing your sacred purpose. When you embody your truest purpose, it becomes a buffer against the madness of the world. No longer ruled by fear and tempted by substitute gratifications, you live a truly authentic life. Your purpose becomes a soul-fulfilling prophecy that reminds you, in every moment, that you have finally made it home.

I am so tired of people saying, "You are exactly where you are supposed to be," no matter what someone's life circumstances and challenges. Yes, there is no question that we can often learn something of value wherever we are on the path; and yes, we may have, in some situations, attracted the exact challenge that we need to grow... BUT that does not mean that we are ALWAYS where we are supposed to be, or that we chose our reality. Telling that to someone in every situation—even when they are ill or suffering tremendously—is arrogant, and adds insult to injury. Sometimes we need a kick in the ass, and sometimes we are just a victim of terrible circumstances. Sometimes we chose our reality, and sometimes it just chose us. Sometimes our suffering is needless and the result of other people's wrongdoing. Compassion demands that we hold the space for other's challenges with a wide-open heart. Let them decide if they are exactly where they are supposed to be. It's not for us to judge.

Timely communication is essential in all forms of relationship. It is also fundamental to the conscious relationship path. If you have an issue with someone's way of relating, express it at the time, or soon thereafter. Give them the benefit of your feelings at a time when they can remember the context and speak to their actions. If you do, there is a very real possibility that they will make an apology and learn how to relate to you in a healthier way. If you don't, there is a very real possibility that your unexpressed feelings will congeal into resentment, ultimately seeping out in a way that undermines the connection altogether. Bottom line— you have a right to be upset with someone. But they also have a right to hear it. There is no substitute for direct and timely communication.

We have to stand for something in this world. We can't just stand for 'looking on the bright side.' There is so much to fight for, so much to stand against. Our silence is complicit. In those moments spent staring at the sun, thousands of injustices occurred. Turn away from the sun, turn towards reality. Humanity needs your boots on the ground. We need every living soul beside us to humanize this mad world. Every single voice. That's what it's going to take.

Think of your triggers as ghosts from your experiential and ancestral history. They are ghosts who have not yet found their peace. They want to—that's why they keep showing up in your life—but they need your help. They need you to get in close and listen, as they share their unresolved past with you. They need you to see them, in just the same way you want to be seen. If you keep ignoring them, they won't go away. They will just show up more often. And your life will become a kind of ghost-fulfilling prophecy, one where every choice you make will haunt your days. Perhaps it's time we accepted that we are the haunted house that we fear. In each room, a ghost that is ready to be liberated. In the basement, the unconscious that is ready to be revealed. We don't need to give ourselves candy on Halloween. We just need to give ourselves permission to heal. That's the sweetest gift of all.

Sometimes playing it safe is playing it unsafe. Especially, in love. You think you're safe, but you're actually putting yourself at risk. Because you aren't exploring your relational depths. You aren't living from your vulnerable edge. You aren't opening your heart. There is something very risky about that. It's too shut down, for your own good. You won't be rejected, but you won't come alive. You won't get burnt, but you won't touch ecstasy. You won't die all alone, but you will live all alone. Sometimes playing it safe is playing it unsafe.

We owe no system our silence. The world is changed by those who speak truth in the face of personal peril. They have every practical reason to go silent, but they simply refuse to cower before it, optics be damned. They stand on the edge of that terrifying abyss, and they speak the whole and bloody truth. They whistle blow when it is against their better interest. Because they realize that no change can happen if we go silent before injustice. The patriarchy has been manipulating our silence for centuries. We owe no man our silence.

I call it the "no responsibility" bypass. It has been perfected by many abusers and manipulators in an effort to sidestep accountability. It comes in many forms: "There are no victims," "You chose these experiences so that you could grow," "That's just another story," "It's all an illusion," "I am just a reflection of you," "Rise above it," and the one I find the most ridiculous: "Why haven't you forgiven ME yet?" In certain circumstances, some of these retorts have a place, but not in those situations where there has been blatant wrongdoing without assuming responsibility. We have swung too far in the direction of a version of "all oneness" that lacks boundaries and common sense. It's not real without them. Boundaries before oneness, localized accountability before the big picture. "I'm sorry," first and foremost.

Thinking you know what's best for someone, isn't what's best for someone. Because you don't know. Only they do, and they are more likely to arrive at the healthiest place for them, when they are accepted exactly as they are. If you can't, then leave them be, and focus on your own life. All that time spent thinking about what's best for someone else, is better spent manifesting what is best for YOU. And when you find it, you will be amazed at how little interest you have in thinking about what's best for someone else. To each their path.

Perpetual Positivity Syndrome (PPS): The addictive need to default to positivity under any and all circumstances. One of the most common obstructions to awakening on the healing path, it prevents a maturation in the deep within because sufferers refuse to be present for all that is. Symptoms include: a constant need to find the light in every situation, a tendency to forget or "rise above" the negative aspects of their partner, an inability to fully support and hold the space for another's suffering, and a turning away from the painstaking work required to meet life's challenges. Instead of forging a grounded, discerning optimism in the grit and grime of daily life— they jump to the light, while averting the shadows that inform it. They habitually bliss-trip, when lessons are waiting in the wings to be integrated and embodied. Those who suffer with PPS are often of the illusory view that they had perfect childhoods or that they have moved beyond the shadow. In most cases, their obsessive clinging to the "positive" is rooted in their own unresolved emotional material: pain and anger that will only come back to haunt them. At the end of the day, there can be no light without shadow, and no substitute for hard-earned transformation.

No one is ordinary. No one is plain. No one is run-of-the-mill. These are disparaging terms that reflect and perpetuate a shamed collective. In fact, every one of us is unique. Every one of us is extraordinary. Every one of us has a precious offering. Our work—in this lifetime and the lifetimes to come—is to get out from under the collective bushel of shame, and treasure ourselves and each other. So much of the destruction on this planet originates in self-judgement. Let's turn that around. Let's begin each day by looking in the mirror and honoring the precious being before us... "I treasure you." And then, let's find at least one person every day that we can offer the same reflection to: "YOU ARE A TREASURE."

However love arrives at your door, it is always a brave path. It is like taking a long walk in a deep dark forest and never quite knowing where your soul will land. It isn't for the faint of heart, nor is it ever to be taken lightly. Real love is heartcore. You have to be tenacious. You have to be innovative. You have to be willing to drop to your knees time and again before its wisdom. And you have to forge the tools you will need from your own imaginings, as very few who have walked the path before can describe the terrain. Most fell into quicksand soon after the romantic phase ended. Relationship is always a spiritual practice, even when we imagine it otherwise.

People who can't find ecstasy in the heart of daily experience, often seek it outside themselves. I see this everywhere I look. There is often a directly proportional relationship between one's hunger for bliss and one's degree of emotional toxicity. The more extreme the internalized pain, the more extreme the quest for externalized bliss. I call them 'bliss-seeking missiles.' Often trauma survivors on the run, they try any drug or extreme experience, in the hopes of tasting from the ecstasy tree. They want it and need it that badly. They are looking for proof that there is more to this life than darkness. They are seeking evidence of essence, anywhere they can find it. This can work, if the energy generated from their adventures is brought back down into the body to work through their stuff. To clear so much emotional and energetic debris that they can one day feel ecstasy naturally, in the heart of daily life. It doesn't work when the bliss-quest becomes an entrenched way of being that floats them further and further way from themselves. Because ecstasy doesn't mean a thing if there isn't an intact self to come home to. The real ecstatic alchemy begins and ends within the self, itself. Centered. Spacious. Ecstatic in the heart of the everything.

The nature of awakening is not transcendence.
It is not detachment.
It is not leaving our bodies.
It is not dismissing our shadow.
It is not disparaging the ego.
It is not feigned positivity.
It is not bashing our story.
It is not new age mysticism.

The nature of awakening is inclusivity.
It is connectiveness.
It is shadow and light.
It is enheartened presence.
And presence is not to be found
on the skyways of self-avoidance.
Presence is to be found right down here,
in our aging body temples,
sole to soul on Mother Earth.

Awakening requires that we show up for all of it.
The great in-wakening.
The holy wholly.

If there is one thing that I am sure of, it is that our past is always with us. It's in our cells, our responses, our patterning. The question is whether it is with us as an obstruction to the moment, or as its seamless foundation. There is much to be said for making 'getting caught up with ourselves' our first priority when we have free time. That is, working through whatever is still lying in wait within us, until we feel unencumbered. Until we feel a freshness of appreciation. There is nothing on our to-do list of greater significance. Moving it through, moving it along, moving it on out...

Most of us have had our fill of people telling us who we are, how we 'should' see things, what we 'should' do in various situations. It's like an unstoppable locomotive of human know-it-all-ness that masquerades as benevolent support. It isn't, unless it is directly asked for. It's one thing to ask someone for their perspective on your situation—it's quite another for them to hurl it at you uninvited. That seldom helps. What does help, is holding the space for another's situation with real-time presence. Listening close, inquiring into their experience, and—if you feel that you have a perspective to offer—asking them if they are interested in exploring it. If they aren't, leave it be and understand that just being there with them, is the best way to support them. You may feel powerless, but you aren't—your presence empowers them. Yes, insight CAN be helpful at times, but presence is ALWAYS helpful. Because what most of us need is to feel accepted by those we share with. Not fixed, not corrected, not 'should on.' ACCEPTED. And, ironically, it is that feeling of acceptance that opens the door to new perspectives. Not because you told them what to think, but because your loving presence made them feel safe enough to think differently. People don't care what you know, but they do know when you care.

Our survival adaptations are so tough, but our wounds are so delicate. To heal, we have to lift the armor carefully—it saved our lives, after all. It's like moving your best friend off to the side of the path. You don't trample her, you don't hit him with a sledgehammer. You honor her presence like a warm blanket that has kept you safe and sound during wintry times. And then, when the moment is right, you get inside and stitch your wounds with the thread of love, slowly and surely, not rushing to completion, nurturing as you weave, tender and true. The healing process has a heart of its own, moving at its own delicate pace. We are such wondrous weavers...

Conscious relationship is not a badge of honor. It's not something you boast about. Nor is it something that you ever fully complete. It's a commitment to relationship as a transformative practice. It's a pledge to stand in the fire of relatedness, even when it burns. And it's the willingness to grow in wisdom on the bridge between your hearts.

We can't thrive, if we don't survive. This may seem obvious, but is sometimes forgotten by those of us on a spiritual path. We forget the ground, and jump into awakening with all our heart. And then, we come crashing back to earth when the money runs out, or when we realize that we forgot to honor our foundational needs. We aren't birds. We're human. We need our roots sturdy and strong, before we can fly. And if we get them solid, we don't even need to fly to awaken. We do it from deep within the ground of our being. On the earth plane. In this divinely constructed body. And from here, we recognize that what we imagined as awakening was often just a flight of fancy. Because sustainable awakening happens from deep within a grounded consciousness. From a place of integration and inclusivity. From sole to soul…

In a kind of lame effort to stand our ground, we used to say, "Sticks and stones may break my bones, but words will never hurt me." But we have come to know how untrue this is. Verbal abuse is violence. It's bullying. It's assaultive. And it can ravage the psyche of those who are attacked. It's high time we stopped pretending that what we say is less destructive than what we do. New languaging would be a good start: "Sticks and stones may break my bones, and words will also hurt me." Because a wound is a wound… is a wound. And the intention to harm comes in many different forms.

There is a strong relationship between the building of our self-esteem, and our willingness to own our buried feelings. When we grant ourselves permission to do the deeper work, we assert our right to exist. We prove to our beaten-down inner child that they matter. This energizes them, and builds their sense of self. Therapy is not just a healing journey. It is also a re-building journey. Every time we cry unshed tears and express buried anger, we strengthen and empower ourselves. We roar ourselves into existence.

We all know that relationships won't develop if one party is easily enraged. At the same time, it's also very difficult for relationships to develop if one or both individuals cannot express their anger and resentments, without someone running away. I once had a dear friend who was so afraid of conflict that he would go silent or flee the connection when he felt angry. He just couldn't find the courage to stand in the fire and work it through. As a result, the connection endured years feigning kindness while walking on eggshells, rather than growing to the next level of intimacy. It's one thing to refuse abusiveness in a connection, but quite another to flee every form of conflict. Sometimes, where there's smoke, there's transformation. But it takes courage to see it through.

If someone says that they were traumatized, they were traumatized. It's that simple. Trauma is a subjective experience. It makes no difference if you can relate to their experience, or if it fits into culturally approved trauma categories. What matters is that the person identified their experience as a trauma. That's all we need to know. If we can move our compassion needle in this direction, we will truly change the world.

I grew up in a home where you were made to suffer for every reward. You didn't get rewarded because you were a child, or because you were a delight, or because you were a worthy human. You got rewarded because you suffered for it. If you grew up in a family like that, be watchful for your own tendency to make your blessings conditional on your suffering. It's an unconscious pattern, one that sometimes takes a deep look before you can see it. But when you do see it, and finally do the work to release the pattern, you can claim your rightful entitlement as a deserving one. You can relish the blessing that you are. You don't have to pay a price to enjoy this life. You can have all the joy you want for free.

Until we stop blaming the mind—and recognize that our anxieties stem from our unresolved emotional body—there will be no liberation.

"God does not give you more than you can handle." Really? Did you ask God yourself? Did she confirm your theory? Look, I get that sometimes we say stuff like this because we don't know what else to say, or because we actually think it helps. We don't want people to give up. We want them to keep on fighting to stay alive. But, honestly, it doesn't help. Few survivalist mantras do. Because there is more to life than survival at all costs. There is more to life than armoring up and toughing it out in the heart of our suffering. There is also something to be said for healing our way to wholeness. For meeting each other in our woundedness. For embracing the possibility that our trauma is actually a lot more than we handle. So, next time you feel tempted to tell a trauma survivor, "God does not give you more than you can handle," try something different. Say this, "Something tragic has happened. You should not have to handle it alone. How can I help you to grieve and to heal?" Remind them that God is a soft place to land. Remind them that God is compassion in human form.

The gurus didn't go to sit in the meditation cave to enlighten their consciousness. They went there to bypass their issues with the world. They didn't turn to silence to extinguish the monkey mind. They turned to silence to turn down the volume on their pain (the monkey heart). They didn't nestle into stillness because stillness is THE royal road to the kingdom of God. They nestled into stillness because movement ignited their triggers and traumas. They didn't dissolve the ego because the ego is the enemy of the sacred. They (allegedly) dissolved the ego because it reminded them of their unresolved humanness. They didn't purify the body because the body is something less than Divine. They purified the body in an effort to escape their emotional toxicity. They didn't strive for transcendence because there is a kingdom up there for us. They strove for transcendence because they lacked the courage to live on Mother Earth. They didn't seek formlessness because it is our most awakened state of being. They sought formlessness because their form hurt too much. They didn't shun anger because anger is a sub-standard emotion. They shunned anger because it uncovered their mountains of grief. They didn't practice non-attachment because non-attachment is the essence of self-realization. They practiced it so they could hide from the challenges of human relationship. They didn't fixate on forgiveness because forgiveness is necessary for a life well-lived. They fixated on forgiveness in order to repress the unforgivable. They didn't preach non-judgment because they aren't actually judgmental. They preached non-judgment so that they could get away with anything.

My friends, we have been fooled for centuries. The patriarchy went to a lot of trouble to cloak and camouflage their personal issues behind a wall of faux awakening. A whole spiritual lineage was birthed from their self-avoidance. And it is now time to call it all out. It is now time to bury patriarchal spirituality in a graveyard of its own making, and to co-create a spirituality that is grounded in our humanness, our bodies, our feelings, our relationships with each other and Mother Earth. This is the only way to save our species.

You should be more afraid of avoiding your path than walking it.

I used to wonder how people could live with themselves after committing crimes against others. But I no longer do. Because what I came to understand is that they aren't actually 'living.' In order to move forward with the knowledge of their complicity, they actually have to sever some part of their aliveness. To some extent, their heart has to close, their presence has to diminish, and their capacity for wholeness has to become obstructed. They may have no conscious awareness of how this happens, but it does happen. In order to live with what they have done, they have to become significantly less alive. Because we are relational beings, we can't bypass the suffering we have caused. It leaves its footprints on every part of our life. The only remedy is for them to bravely own their actions, and to genuinely make amends. Otherwise, the crime lives on and on....

Healing isn't a short-term process. It's a long-term practice. Because it's not just about healing the wound itself. It's also about retrieving what has been lost, integrating new parts, maturing in the places that the trauma obstructed. It's about developing into the truest version of yourself possible, after years buried below the weight of adaptation and disguise. It's about catching up with yourself, after years on the run. Healing is a life-long practice.

It doesn't matter what people think about what you express. It matters that you express it. And the more brazen and true your voice, the more attacks will come your way. This is utterly inevitable. You must know this going in. And you must continue to find and assert your voice. Because it is the true voice that will save us from ourselves. Without it, we are lost, lost, lost. Speak your bravest voice, always. The more they attack, the more you express. The more they resist, the more you persist. The more attention they give you, the more attention you give you. Use their hostility as fodder for your own empowerment. Use it to nourish your self-concept and strengthen your resolve. Put it on your cereal, and eat them whole.

Not everyone is born to partner. And those who aren't, should never be shamed or shunned because they take a different path. In fact, our world would be much worse off without them. Many are here with a more individuated calling. Some are born to explore the interior realms, independent of relational challenges. Others, to create brilliant and beautiful things, with little to distract them. And others have been so wounded by relationship that they feel safer and happier on their own. Whatever it is, the assumption that partnership is the measure of an actualized life is misguided. Every soul has a unique path to walk. The measure of a life well-lived is whether we walk it.

I think of the children often, those who are trapped in terribly challenging circumstances, and how important it is to notice them, to empower them, to listen to them. I think of how little love it can take to inspire them to believe in life again, when nothing in their immediate environment nourishes them. If they have just a little bit of light to warm them, they can go on and overcome their circumstances. May we be the light for those young people who need it until they can claim it as their own. A little attention, a moment of attunement, a simple compliment, can save a life. It only takes a little to change everything.

The highest thing is the truest thing.
The truest thing is the highest thing.

They say it takes "two to tango" when people describe a relational conflict. Well, actually, it takes two hundred, two thousand, two million to tango. We are all composites of the ancestral trauma and unhealthy patterns that preceded us. That's not to say that there aren't victims of aggression in certain dynamics—abusers must always be held accountable for their actions—but it is to say that so much of what happens in relationships is a function of everything, and everyone, that has come before. To really understand what is happening, and to finally reach a stage where change is possible, we must go back in time and make sense of where we came from. We must come to understand the ways that our lineage shapes our behavior and influences our choices. If we don't do this work, then we can be certain of one thing in this lifetime—nothing will change. We will continue to perpetuate the unhealthy cycles of those who came before, and to pass them on—like a toxic torch—to those that follow. If you want a healthier future, you have to first go back in time...

No wonder there is confusion in transformational communities. The (grounded) psychotherapeutic movement encourages the development of the healthy ego. The (ungrounded) spiritual movement glorifies the dissolution of the ego. The psychotherapeutic movement invites us to individuate and develop healthy boundaries. The spiritual movement insists that we eradicate boundaries in the name of 'Oneness.' The psychotherapeutic movement encourages us to develop the uniquely individuated self. The spiritual movement asserts that there is no self. The psychological movement invites us to speak and honor our stories. The spiritual movement denies their significance, and insists that we 'turn them around' until they become something else. The psychotherapeutic movement invites us to find our answers in our bodies, down here on Mother Earth. The ungrounded spirituality movement encourages us to find our answers in the transcendence emptiness, flying high in Father Sky. The psychotherapeutic movement encourages us to forgive abusers, only if forgiveness arises organically. The spiritual movement demands that we forgive at all costs, as a measure of our spiritual value. The psychotherapeutic movement believes that our feelings, and this whole bloodied human trip, are entirely real. The ungrounded spiritual movement teaches us that it's all an illusion—every bit of it.

No wonder healers and seekers feel confused. These are two entirely different frameworks of perception. And one of them is not leading us anywhere good.

I once had a friend who only ever wanted to talk about me. They were wonderful at asking me questions, and holding the space for my story. But they would never talk about themselves, no matter how often I inquired. At first, I loved the opportunity to be heard, but then I began to feel used. It felt like I was actually serving a psychological purpose for them. I was enabling them in their self-avoidance. Bottom line… When all we do is hold the space for one person's experience, no friendship can truly form. Because friendships can't be one-way streets. They need two lanes to flourish. Two sharers, and two listeners, growing in closeness over time.

Contrary to some New Cage teachings, acceptance does NOT mean pretending to love something we don't. It means accepting that it happened, and allowing whatever feelings arise. Love may not be one of them. What is most important is that we are true to how we feel—not doing the smiley-faced bliss bypass, not feigning unconditional love and premature forgiveness, not jumping to witnessing in an effort to avoid the pain—but truly allowing ourselves to surrender to the feelings and move them through to transformation. No fake smiles, no dissociative head-trips—just surrender and release. The world has been seeking band-aid solutions to real problems for centuries. There aren't any. We need to get real with the feel if we are going to heal.

If you want to live a more spiritual life,
live a more human life. Be more truly,
fiercely, heartfully human.

The thing we often forget regarding our own changes and others' changes is that real transformation takes real time. No matter how eager we are to see things shift and grow, it will seldom happen rapidly. This is particularly true with respect to emotional maturation. It is often a many-years-long journey to empty these crowded vessels. Developmental stages are like biological structures. To move from one stage of maturation to another, we have to go through a broad range of experiences, integrate their meaning, and try a new way of being on for size. It is about becoming a truly different being on many interconnected levels. I spent a lot of years in hurry-up offense with my own transformation and those around me. It was a waste of time. Sustainable change is built on a foundation of patience. Persistence and patience.

All too often, freedom is confused with escape. As in 'freedom from' something… freedom from society, freedom from family, freedom from authority. This was my idea of freedom for many years, but then it began to feel like a strangely constricted prison. One where I could only feel free if I was running from or to something. One where I needed a very particular set of circumstances to make me feel safe. And then it occurred to me that I didn't know a thing about freedom. I had escaped, but I wasn't free. Because real freedom isn't an act of rebellion. It's not a flight of fancy. It's about finding freedom at the heart of the everything. It's about feeling free everywhere. Free at last.

Everything happens for a reason,
but it's not always a good one.

Fatemates: Those individuals who are fated to encounter each other in this lifetime. Members of the same soulpod, their meeting was pre-destined, encoded in their sacred blueprint, fundamental to their expansion in this lifetime. Although they were fated to connect, the deeper challenge is clarifying the reasons why. Contrary to the popular myth that fatemates are meant to spend their lives happily together, the opposite is often true. Some are destined to travel together through time; others are destined to share the briefest of encounters before moving onto the next pop-up on the path. Some are meant to expand together joyfully; others to polish the rough diamond of the soul by triggering and challenging each other. The serendipity that brings them together is often easy to spot—interpreting it is the real art form. We all have a date with fate—the question is what direction it will take us...

We cannot measure our life accomplishments by comparing ourselves to others. When we try to, most of us feel immobilized by comparison. Because there is no objective standard by which to measure success. There is always someone who seems to have achieved more than we have. The real way to measure accomplishment is subjectively, by reference to the subtleties of personal context. That is, what have you had to overcome emotionally, relationally, physically, and structurally, in order to make your way through life? What did it take to get where you are? I know many so-called "great achievers" who had a leg up at every turn. While many unknown people have achieved far more by working diligently in the deep within to transform their individual and ancestral landscape. From the place they come, their small steps are momentous and (r)evolutionary. So, if you are shackled by your perception of someone else's accomplishments, throw comparison to the wind. Stand up before yourself and applaud how far you have come. It may not be anything you can ever put to words. But you know. YOU KNOW.

Don't fight for the facade, the feigned, the fake. Fight for the authentic, the genuine, the real. Truth is the prayer that will transform the species. Truth is the path to collective healing. Truth is the ONLY way home. Speak it now, before it's too late.

I grew up in a home where love was measured by abuse. Not only did they abuse those they loved, but they measured our love for them by the amount of pain we were willing to endure at their hands. Talk about a recipe for disaster in later life, where pure, vulnerable love appeared suspicious by contrast, and abusive relationships felt oddly safe. Little did they know that our willingness to endure their abuse was not a measure of love—it was a reflection of our self-hatred. You don't endure abuse because you love someone—you endure it because you don't love yourself. Once you do the work to regain your sense of worth, abuse becomes an impossible path.

I have known many famous people. Few of them understood the secret of life. Most were so trapped inside of their childhood need for attention that they never graduated to the next stage. That stage is very profound and very private. It's the stage where the "little voice that knows" calls to you, lovingly reminding you of your one true path. Not the path that demands the most attention, but the path that threads right through the heart of your soul. There's a path in there with your name on it, and it longs to be lived. And when you live it, you no longer need to chase the world. You no longer crave applause. Because home is where the soul is. One soul clapping is more than enough.

My soul won't rest until everybody is safe and sound(ing). We have been frightened and repressed for far too long. Abusers of power begone. It's time for all humans to express themselves fully and rise into fullness.

Sometimes people walk away from love because it is so beautiful that it terrifies them. Sometimes they leave because the connection shines a bright light on their dark places and they are not ready to work them through. Sometimes they run away because they are not developmentally prepared to merge with another—they have more individuation work to do first. Sometimes they take off because love is not a priority in their lives—they have another path and purpose to walk first. Sometimes they end it because they prefer a relationship that is more practical than conscious, one that does not threaten the ways that they organize reality. Because so many of us carry shame, we have a tendency to personalize love's leavings, triggered by the rejection and feelings of abandonment. But this is not always true. Sometimes it has nothing to do with us. Sometimes the one who leaves is just not ready to hold it safe. Sometimes they know something we don't—they know their limits at that moment in time. Real love is no easy path—readiness is everything. May we grieve loss without personalizing it. May we learn to love ourselves in the absence of the lover.

Your calling isn't something distinct from your emotional healing. It is synonymous with it. At this stage of human development, it is all many of us can do to excavate and heal our ancestral and personal trauma. There is just so much of it. And the healing of it is not blocking your path. It is your path. If you spend your whole life healing even a small portion of it, you have lived a luminous life, infused with sacred purpose. You have done something that perhaps no one in your lineage has ever done before: HEALING. There is no calling more noble, no path more honorable, no step more profound. So don't beat yourself up, if you can't get to that lofty offering you want to bring to the world. Because you are already doing the greatest thing of all: HEALING HUMANITY. Thank you.

Knowing our issues is not the same as healing our issues. Your emotional material does not evaporate because you watch it. I have known many who could watch and name their patterns and issues as if they were scientists, researching their own consciousness, but nothing fundamentally changed, because they refused to come back down into their bodies and move their feelings through to transformation. It's safe up there, above the fray, witnessing the pain-body without actually engaging it. Yes, you may be able to develop certain techniques that detach your awareness from your pain. You may be able to become so skilled at a witnessing consciousness that you can overpower your triggers. But that's not presence. Real presence comes through the open heart.

The key to the transformation of challenging patterns and wounds is to heal them from the inside out. Not to analyze them, not to watch them like an astronomer staring at a faraway planet through a telescope, but to jump right into the heart of them, encouraging their expression and release, stitching them into new possibilities with the thread of love. You want to live a holy life? Heal your heart. That's the best meditation of all.

I understand some of the reasoning behind inviting people not to see themselves as victims in certain situations where they have suffered or been abused. We want to empower them and support them to move beyond the negativity associated with victim self-identification. BUT it is my view that this shift—from victimization to empowerment—is a PROCESS that often first requires a recognition of the ways we have been victimized. So many on this planet have endured horrors that they have yet to even express and heal from. Let's start there. You have to acknowledge yourself as a victim before you recognize the karmic choices you may have made to become one. The lesson—if there is one— begins with a self-dignifying recognition of the wrong that was committed. Let's start there, and embrace that truth deeply, before inviting people to jump to platitudes such as: 'karmic contract,' and 'lesson,' and 'It was a blessing in disguise.' First, it was an abuse. Let's heal that first.

The most significant relationships are the ones that bring us restoration. Restoration of our hope, our aliveness, our missing pieces. When we encounter them, we feel ourselves return to wholeness. These are the relationships we need.

Sincere apology changes everything. Not politically motivated apologies, not agenda-driven apologies, not apologies rooted in fear. Genuine apologies. The kind that come right through the heart. The kind you can't help but make. The real ones.

It can be very difficult for pragmatic people to understand those who are soul-driven. Because pragmatists weigh decisions primarily on the basis of tangible outcomes. That is, is this step more or less likely to lead to material benefit and a greater sense of security in the world? If it doesn't resonate with their version of common sense, they reject it. But soul-driven people operate differently. They may integrate practicality into some of their decisions, but they prioritize the soul's journey above all else. They see themselves as a soul on a journey through time(less), and they ground their most significant decisions in their soul's trajectory: What does my soul say about the direction I need to walk? Will this step catalyze, or neutralize, my soul's evolution? Does it reflect the next stage of my soulular development, or is it a step backwards? Is this evolution or devolution? This is often the reason why people around us don't get us. We are dancing to an entirely different beat. The soul has a rhythm all its own.

There is a kind of narcissism at the heart of some empathic tendencies. I learned this with myself. I had a tendency to listen to people's traumatic stories with an empathic ear, trying to relate what they were telling me to my own experience. There was a healthy aspect to this—I was trying to make their stories real for me. But there was a very self-absorbed aspect to this, too. Because if I couldn't empathize, there was a way in which I didn't believe their story to be true. In other words, if I couldn't relate, it wasn't as real for me. And that was the problem. I was making the truthfulness of their story dependent on my personal experience. In other words, it became all about me. Rather than just truly, deeply listening, and believing them even if I couldn't relate. Our compassion shouldn't be dependent on whether we can relate to another's suffering. If it's real for them, it's real.

It is natural to take it personally when someone disconnects from you, especially when they don't tell you why. At the same time, it is also important to realize that someone's decision to disconnect often has nothing to do with you. It is often entirely about them. One of the most common things I have witnessed, is a need to sever connection that is rooted in the personal individuation process. Someone has gone through their life as a people-pleaser, as a co-dependent, as someone whose experience of the self is confusingly enmeshed with others, and they need to push someone away in order to finally feel separate. They need to claim their stake as an individuated entity, but they don't know how to do it non-reactively. So, they abruptly terminate a personal connection in order to establish a new way of being. Quite often, they do this with someone who is peripheral to their primary co-dependencies, because they are not yet ready to live without those. They pick a friend or a secondary figure, as their first break-away. In these situations, you are merely a relational symbology, a figure that had to go in order for them to finally feel like a boundaried, empowered person. This is not to say that it won't hurt, but it is to say that it was never about you.

Some trauma histories mix better than others. This is a primary reason why some relationships flourish, and others don't. Some trigger patterns coalesce well, while others just get worse. A conscious intention to heal together can go a long way, but it's not always enough. Not because you are wounded people, but because your stuff and their stuff don't blend well. This isn't something to beat yourself up for. We are all trauma survivors, to one degree or another. We can't feel safe with just anyone. Our traumas have to align. If love relationship is a priority for you, the trick is to find someone with a trauma history that is compatible with yours. Not just tolerating each other's stuff, but actually healing and transforming it together. This is the key to relationship success in a traumatized world.

Giving restores our faith.
Giving builds bridges.
Giving opens hearts.
Giving connects us to source.
Giving tears down walls.
Giving reminds us that we are not alone.

No matter how bad it gets,
Don't give up.

Give.

It will remind you of your own significance.

They call themselves therapists, but sometimes they aren't about healing at all. They're about avoiding. With little more than 'It's all Good' and 'Perpetual Positivity Syndrome' in their toolbox, they steer you away from your unresolved trauma, just like they steered themselves away from theirs. A therapist can only take you as far as they have gone. And if they are still stuck in a faux positivity loop, they will do everything they can to bring you there, too. Because hovering above the pain is where they live. Because their habitual range of emotion is restricted to their comfort zone. Beware the avoidapist who is more comfortable in the shallows than the depths. They will waste your precious time and f*ck you up good. Find the therapist who has walked the deep road, and who can accompany you on your journey. That's the one you want.

It's not the darkness that scares me. It's the darkness hiding behind the light. It's the shadow camouflaged as transparency. It's the manipulations hiding behind a smiley-faced emoji. It's the ambition feigning as altruism. It's not the darkness that scares me. It's the lie.

When people tell you what they think you should do in a situation, what they are usually telling you is what they think they would do. Because they can't really know what you should do, unless they are walking in your shoes. And if they are, they will likely do whatever it is that you end up doing, because that's what it means to truly walk in someone's shoes. You see the world through their eyes. To avoid this conundrum altogether, don't tell people what they should do in their situation. Support them in figuring it out for themselves.

In love relationship, there are openers, and there are closers. It's important to understand the difference. Openers are expert at cracking your heart open. They are masters of seduction and specialize in the early stages of romantic love. But they never stay the course. They exit as soon as the triggers enter. Closers are a different kind of lover. They can open, but they are also committed to closing the deal—even if it takes years of hard work to get it right. They are there for the long haul. If you are looking for lasting love, be on the lookout for the closers. And close the door on the openers. Time is of the essence.

One of the ways that humanity is controlled and contained is by manipulating us to live vicariously through the 'cool,' the hip, the glamorous, the rich, the famous. Celebrity culture is fundamental to predatory marketing constructs. The more identified we are with the projections of someone else's allegedly amazing life, the more disidentified we are with our own. And then the easier it is to get us to purchase the products and magic bullets that benefit only them. At its heart, predatory consumerism targets the uncentered, the self-hating, the shamed. The more diminished our self-concept, the more susceptible we are to live our lives vicariously. In our efforts to equalize human worth, we must deconstruct this little game. We must turn away from the illusion that someone else's life has more value, and wholeheartedly embrace our own. Forget the rich and famous. YOUR life is your path. The beautiful path of you.

The path of self-creation is not for the faint of soul. It will take everything you've got to overcome misguided cultural conditioning and seemingly impossible circumstances. And, even then, you will have to contend with your own internalized shame and self-doubt. It's an uncomfortable adventure that will stretch your consciousness well beyond its habitual range of e-motion. And yet, do you really have a choice? Isn't that why you are here?

You don't ask for every bad thing that happens to you. You may learn from it in some cases, but that still doesn't mean you asked for it. Telling someone who has been traumatized that they asked for it on some karmic level is shaming and hurtful. They alone can decide if they invited it in—they don't need to hear it from others. They need to hear your compassion.

It is one thing to try to live with an open heart, but it is quite another to keep your heart open with those who have hurt you. I do not believe that the latter is healthy, sensible, or necessary. Instead, practice the art of conscious armoring when confronted with hurtful people. Don't grant them the power to close your heart altogether. Protect it when you are in their company. Make a conscious decision to armor it while interacting with them, and to then re-open it as soon as the coast is clear. And, ultimately, practice the art of selective attachment wherever possible. That is, only open your heart to those who have proven that they are loving and safe. Give yourself the love you deserve, by granting yourself the right to open, or to close, as circumstances require. You are under no obligation to suffer at another's hands. Your heart is not theirs for the taking. It's yours for the loving.

Shifting from a co-dependent tendency to one that is healthily dependent is no easy path. If your habitual pattern of relating is to fuse to another, it can be excruciating to know reality without it. Merging has become your experience of love, and anything else feels unnatural, perhaps even terrifying. And yet, the only way to truly love another is from one step back. If you're in too close, you can't see them, and they can't see you. You think you're in love, but you aren't You're in need. Because you can't love someone you can't see. So take a step back energetically and emotionally, and look closer at the person you are bonded to. Let them breathe into their separateness. And you breathe into yours. Now watch love take root on the bridge between your hearts.

I have often found it interesting that those who are comfortable with the healthy expression of their anger, often have far less conflict in their lives, than those who shame and shun anger. In my experience, the anger shamers are often overwhelmed with inner conflict, and their personal lives are littered with misplaced aggression and rage. Their repression of their own anger made it impossible for them to live without it. It's everywhere they step...

"Should I stay or should I go?" Good question, but perhaps there is a better way to ask it…"Should I stay or should I grow?" If we ask it this way, we have something to guide our inquiry. Not that we can't stay and grow, but sometimes, we can only grow if we go. If that's the case, then you don't have much of a choice. Go, and grow.

It's none of anyone's business if someone chooses to identify with their victimhood for a day, a year, or a lifetime. Victimhood has no time limit. And if it does, it's for the victim to determine. It's one thing to say that you have moved beyond your own victimhood, but don't be speaking for all of humanity. You didn't walk in everyone's shoes. Some people have been so traumatized that they can't (and won't) even get out of bed. They are the casualties of a still-insensitive world. It's not for us to judge them. It's not for us to tell them what steps to take. It's for us to meet them right where they are.

You don't need a guru to tell you what your path is. You don't need the Akashic records to clarify your course. You just need to clear the emotional debris that obstructs your knowing. You just need to peel away the layers of misidentification. You just need to look inside of your beautiful bones. Your true-path is encoded within you, living at the core of your being. There it is, waiting for its opportunity to be excavated and humanifested. Helpers can support the clearing, but they cannot know the path you are here to walk. They cannot read from your unique soul-scriptures. Only you can.

The changes that we long for individually and collectively demand that we ReBrave after generations of our courage torn asunder. Presently, I am ReBraving after a difficult stage that un-braved me. It is evident to me that many of the systems that govern and manage us are actually designed to un-brave us. Because if we are not brave, we will not see the ways that we are worked and manipulated. And we will not speak truth to power. A ReBraved humanity will not tolerate anything that impedes our gifts, callings, and offerings. A ReBraved humanity will burn through the veils of greed and deception that obstruct us. A ReBraved humanity will craft the world of limitless possibility that is our individual and collective birthright. A ReBraved humanity will fight for our right to the light. A ReBraved humanity cannot be stopped.

I always wanted to die a warrior, on the battlefield of truth. I can think of no greater cause. I dedicate the rest of my life to ReBraving myself and others. We have been diminished and disempowered for far too long. Join me, if you will.

A difficult love relationship is no gift, but it may be a psychological necessity. Not because suffering is the only path to growth, but because we're at a stage—as a species—where we often need to learn the hard way. This is particularly true with respect to love relationship. Very few of us grew up with anything approaching healthy relatedness. Our ancestors were trapped inside of centuries of generational dysfunction. They had no clue. So, it's left to us to figure it out. We are the pioneers of a new way of relating. The key is to not beat yourself up when love gets difficult. Instead, see it as a laboratory for your own expansion. You are forging the tools you need from your own imaginings. One lesson at a time…

There is so much suffering in the world. Sometimes I wonder how the earth holds it all. And then I see someone who has endured so much find their way through the pain tunnel to a truly better place. I am not talking about the bypassing of the pain-body. I am talking about the courageous working through of the emotional debris. And then I marvel at the human spirit, which creates whatever tools it needs to overcome the odds and find its way home. Wow. Humans. Wow.

I recognize that we have evolved beyond the point where we turn away from everyone that triggers us. We have come to understand that, sometimes, the trigger points us back in the direction of unhealed material that seeks resolution. The willingness to hang in there with this dynamic, and to work through the revealed material, can be fundamental to our expansion. Unfortunately, this practice can be taken much too far and become a recipe for masochistic self-destruction. Not everything that feels painful in a relationship is a gift. Not every trigger is a function of our limitations. Not every disturbing reflection is a helpful mirror. Sometimes it is, and sometimes it's a reminder that you need better boundaries. Sometimes it means that you are simply not where you belong. Working through our stuff doesn't always mean that we hang in there and suffer. Sometimes it means that we take the next exit.

If we don't look at the relationship between our childhood trauma and our ways of being, we will never grow into adulthood. We imagine ourselves liberated from trauma, but our trauma is running the show. Every single person I have known who was fixated on oneness, awakening, transcendence, and enlightenment, was fleeing an unresolved childhood. These flights of fancy were essential coping strategies, but eventually came crashing down to earth. Because there can be no awakening without healing, no oneness without integration, no transcendence without embodiment. And when you actually do that work, the most amazing thing happens. You stop looking for it out there, or up there. You find it right here, in the bones of your being. Breathing in, breathing out, here we are.

People spend so much time protecting the unreal, defending the meaningless, fighting for realities that don't actually serve them. Sometimes they devote their entire lives to these distractions and diversions. Meanwhile, that which is real waits for them with bated breath, not remotely interested in anything inauthentic. We are only here for a moment. Make every second real.

You can't answer all your questions about your path at once. You just can't. And if you try to, you will end up answering none of them. You will just be more confused than when you began. Because the questions have an intrinsic order to them. They build upon each other. For example, you probably can't answer the question of your ultimate calling while you are still confused about how to heal from your trauma. It simply isn't possible to see the path in its entirety, when there are still mountains of emotional debris in the way. First things, first. It can be helpful to write all your life goals down, but stay with the goal that truly matters right now. Stay focused on the stage you are at, before seeking to address the next stage of inquiry. If you do it this way, you will unfold at the precise pace that you should. You will arrive at your own door, right when you are ready to open it.

When confronted with people judging your experience, please remember this: The truthfulness of your experience is not determined by how it is measured, judged, or perceived by another. It stands alone, as a lived experience. People's opinions are often meaningless reflections of their own filters and projections. Nothing to do with the events that occurred. Nothing to do with what was real, for you. It is just their story superimposed onto yours. In fact, no one can take the real from you. No one. So, when they try to whittle you down with their version of YOUR reality, remind them that your lived experience is not up for debate. It's yours and yours alone.

There's nothing free about non-commitment rooted in intimacy avoidance. There's nothing free about polyamory emanating from unresolved trauma history. There's nothing free about wanderlust sourced in relational terror. Being a 'free spirit' has its place—as part of the exploration of self, other, relationship, and alternative ways of being. But if it's emanating from woundedness, it's just another prison. Our defenses can trick us into believing that our hunger for freedom is fundamental to our soul's imprint, but it's often something else. It's often an ungrounded flight of fancy, a delay tactic, a hide-and-seek game we are playing with our pain. If we avoid closeness, we can fool ourselves into believing that we have healed. But it only works for so long. Because we aren't healed, and the remnants of our unresolved pain will show up everywhere. Simply put, we are wounded in close relationship, and some part of our healing has to happen in close relationship. There's no way around it. The best way to free ourselves from pain-body prison is to learn how to trust again.

There's a significant difference between a heart-to-heart conversation, and a projection-to-projection conversation. When we speak to and from the heart, we stand a real chance of making relational progress. Our vulnerabilities are exposed and embraced, and our true feelings rise into view. When we speak from our projections—of self, of other—we are more likely to make things worse. Because projected dynamics are rooted in assumption and misinterpretation. And when we speak from that place, new projections are birthed. Projection begets projection. Vulnerability begets vulnerability. So, if you are planning to have a meaningful conversation with a significant other, spend some time beforehand doing all that you can to see through the veils to what is real. The real you, the real them, the real issues between you. And then connect from that place. Speak from your heart, hear with your heart, inquire from your heart. It may feel scary, but miracles happen when two souls meet on a bridge between their hearts.

I am tired of hearing what normal is from heart-severed head-trippers. I am tired of hearing what normal is from compassionless religious fanatics. I am tired of hearing what normal is from those who shame and shun free expression. I am tired of hearing what normal is from people trapped inside fearful and rigid paradigms.

I want to hear what normal is from courageous inner explorers. I want to hear what normal is from those deeply in their hearts. I want to hear what normal is from those who celebrate authenticity. I want to hear what normal is from those brave pioneers who forge new pathways of possibility for all of us. Normal is a relative concept, one that expands exponentially as we move towards the outer edges of human possibility.

It's not about "letting it go." It's about letting it in. It's about letting it deep. It's about letting it through. It's about being true to your feelings. It's about giving your experiences the attention they deserve. And that may take a moment, or it may take years. The trick is not to shame your need to cling to what is presently unresolved. "Let it go" is the mantra of the self-avoidant, feigning resolution because they lack the courage or the preparedness to face their feelings. Let's not play that game. Let's allow things in and through, until they are fully and truly ready to shift. Let's allow them to grow into the transformation at their heart. We write our story by fully living it. Not by "letting it go" before its time.

Our callings are a life and death matter. When we find them, they infuse us with the light of true-path. They become our portals to divinity, our buffers against the madness of the world. They become our healing balm, our immune boost, our vitamin C! They give us life, and they give life to those we share them with. They truly are the treasure we seek, and the treasure that we must protect with all that we are. Because they are all that we are. Find them, and everything comes to life. Don't find them, and everything turns to dust. Our lives are a treasure hunt, a willful quest for that which lives inside of us. It's all right there, beneath the cobwebs of distortion and distraction, longing to be humanifest. Whatever you seek in life, seek this first. Strive for your callings with all your might. Good will(ful) hunting!

We have a natural tendency to assume that a remarkable chemistry between two souls is confirmation they are meant to be together. In the heat of profound feelings, it seems counter-intuitive to imagine ourselves separate from our beloved. But chemistry and longevity aren't necessarily companions. Just because we feel earth-shatteringly alive with someone doesn't mean they are supposed to be our life partner. They may have come for a very different reason—to awaken us, to expand us, to shatter us so wide open that we can never close again. Perhaps they were sent from afar to polish the rough diamond of our soul before vanishing into eternity. Better we surrender our expectations when the beloved comes. (S)he may just be dropping in for a visit. Is the kettle on?

So many are choosing to leave us right now by their own hand. There are many reasons for this, but some were affixed to the ungrounded spiritualities of the new age, which served them for a time, but then they came crashing back to earth, ill-equipped to manage reality. All those years spent staring at the pain-body across the room while their shadow grew larger, congealing into weapons that turned inward against the self. I will not deny my anger, nor pretend that ungrounded teachings and beliefs did not contribute to their departure. After the pseudo-positivity falls away, after our shunned story reminds us that it is deeply real, after the neglected shadow returns with a vengeance, we need to get support. Not support from the ungrounded spirituality movement, not from new age grifters who sell enlightenment by the bushel, but from grounded healers and therapists who understand the necessity for healing and resolution. When the truth hits the fan, we don't need mantras of self-avoidance. We don't need dissociation techniques. We don't need exorbitantly priced quick fix workshops. We don't need Eastern wisdoms that negate the psyche. We need to be seen and supported. We need to be held in the heart of compassion. We need to heal.

Essential lessons cannot be avoided. Callings don't go away. When we turn away from our lessons, when we ignore our truth-aches, the universe jumps into action, orchestrating our return—a symphony of self-creation dedicated to our unique expansion. This is the nature of karmic gravity—we are returned back to our path until we fully walk it. Return to sender, address now known…

"Suffering builds character!" Really? Is that what it builds? I thought it built walls, armor, anxiety, PTSD. Besides, don't we have enough character already? Or maybe you're talking about a different kind of 'character'—the kind that is forged in the fires of hell. The kind I'm after is a little different. It's built with kindness, tenderness, compassion, pleasure! Perhaps it's time we redefined our understanding of 'character.' And let go of the idea that suffering is a developmental necessity. It isn't. Love is.

You don't have to process because someone else wants you to process. There is an assumption in the therapeutic community, that someone's unwillingness to process is a sign of avoidance. Sometimes it is, and sometimes it isn't. Sometimes, we choose not to process because we don't have the energy. Or because we have other priorities. Or because we don't feel there is anything significant to learn from the experience. Or because we want to process when we are in the just right space to reap its benefits. Or because we just aren't ready. Don't let anyone pressure you into processing. Let it be on your own terms.

We often hear people say, "I cried like a baby," after they listen to or watch something that touches them deeply. Of course, crying is a very good thing, essential for healthy functioning. But it's not just a baby thing. It's also an adult thing. You didn't just "cry like a baby." You also "cried like an adult." And that's a beautiful thing, too. We have been shaming and shunning healthy emotional release for centuries. It's a mark of adulthood to put our feelings away. And it is killing us. So, the next time you have a good cry, make a different kind of pronouncement: "I CRIED LIKE AN ADULT." And then, take it to the next level… "I CRIED LIKE A HUMAN." And set the world free.

It's all coming clear now, isn't it? The ways that we are worked by the economic and political-powers-that-be. All for their benefit. All to our detriment. Wolves in sheep's clothing, everywhere. It seems very evident that we have almost had enough of this sick, sadistic game. It's time to tell the truth about all of it. It's ROARING time. Roaring humanity back to life.

This planet is riddled with victims. Many. Just open your eyes. There is trauma, everywhere. And we aren't going to co-create a more humane world if we keep denying it. Diminishing it. Belittling it. Burying it. This is just victim-bashing. Instead of normalizing repression, we must co-create a world that invites every trauma survivor to share their story fully, and without shame. In so doing, they both heal themselves, and they give permission for everyone else to self-reveal as well. Honest naked vulnerability. Where real healing lies. The collective then begins to heal, and just as importantly, feels ignited to make the kinds of changes—relationally, societally, culturally, and legally—that minimize future traumas. If we keep denying the existence of victimhood, then what will inspire positive change? Nothing.

One of the hallmarks of the ungrounded spiritual movement is this statement: "There is only THIS moment." It is often made by spiritual teachers who are dissociating from their unresolved history: self-avoidance masquerading as enlightenment. We can understand the value of this way of thinking—it calls us out of our worry-mind, our habitual consciousness—and reminds us to be here, now. But it doesn't work—at least not for very long. Because "this moment" actually includes and encompasses every moment before. The past is not behind us—as many of us wish it was—it is deep within us, encoded in our cells, somatized as memory and unresolved trauma. It fully informs our lens on reality. In most cases, the "power of now" is just a dissociative construct. Because most of us are still influenced, and ruled by, the power of "then." The answer is not to pretend we are present, when all we have done is fled or momentarily suspended our past. That's not true presence. That's not true healing. The answer is to own, embody, and resolve the "then," so that our experience of the moment both honors our history and recognizes the ways our moment is informed by our past. It is to recognize that past and present are intrinsic to each other. The mystery begins with our history.

I've always disliked sneaky people. They make the world an unsafe place. It took me a long time before I could spot them, but now I am much better at it. I can see their sneakiness in their eyes, in their dark and distorted energy, in the way they persistently avoid questions. Sneakiness has a visible, somatic imprint. It's almost like it wants to reveal itself. Do you know what I mean?

Don't allow yourself to be held hostage to someone's relationship ambivalence. It's easy to understand why you might—abandonment and rejection issues, fantastical tendencies, mixed messages—but it's important to draw a fine line in the sand. Both so that you don't waste your precious time, and so that you validate your own significance. Waiting on someone to decide how they feel about you, is the ultimate in self-hatred. They can certainly try to connect when they make up their mind, but it is essential to allow yourself to get on with your life, in their absence. Your value exists in and of itself. It doesn't wait on anyone else's approval. And time spent waiting is time far better spent... living.

Home is where the regulation is.

A true master follows their own footprints, encoded within before arriving in this incarnation. Someone else may remind them, someone else may in-power them, but no one else can possibly know the unique contours of their own true-path. Since you are the only one living in your body-temple, only you can know its scriptures and interpretive structure. The next step is right there inside you, divinely imprinted on the souls of your feet.

What one person calls a psychotic break, another calls a break for inner freedom. Sometimes people 'leave reality' because there is an older, incomplete reality that wants to come through to be healed. They can only push it down for so long, before it pushes up against them, demanding to be seen and resolved.

What one person calls reality, another calls a well-mannered lie. Sometimes the most 'well-adjusted' person is the one with the most skeletons in their closet. Sometimes the one with 'mental illness' is the one with the courage to be genuine. Their healing may take years—it can't happen overnight because the material didn't accumulate overnight. But it may be the bravest journey of all.

As we work together to humanize this shaming world, may we seek to understand and support those who are struggling with mental and emotional challenges. They may well be the only ones who can show us how to integrate old realities with new ones. They may be the most honest ones among us. They may well be our trail-blazers for a more authentic life.

Depression is frozen feeling. The best way to heal it is to get to its roots. To get right inside those frozen feelings, and to thaw them out somatically. We felt the initial pain in our hearts. We must go right back inside of our hearts to feel and resolve it. No more damming up of our emotions. No more defenses and denials. Instead, a society-wide acceptance of the fact that we are all carrying pain. There is nothing to be ashamed of. It's intrinsic to our collective experience. And a culturally embraced invitation to do the real work to heal its deep roots with body-centered psychotherapies. And with love. The more we can love those who are struggling with depression, the more strength they will have to reclaim their past and heal their hearts. They didn't have support back then. Let's give it to them, now. Let's create a safe societal container to bring those feelings back to the surface. THE FEEL IS FOR REAL. Let's feel our way back to life...

If we age honestly, we become love. As the body weakens, love surges through us, longing to be released, longing to be lived. With no time left to not love, we seek authentic embrace everywhere. Our deft avoidance maneuvers convert into directness. Our armored hearts melt into pools of eternal longing. This is why we should look forward to aging. Finally, after all the masks and disguises fall away, we are left with love alone. God waits for us on the bridge between our hearts.

Everything begins with acceptance. Even an honorable attempt to suggest another perspective will be met with resistance if someone doesn't feel fundamentally accepted as they are. Because the entire human family has been shamed and diminished. The moment we hear a "should," or a "better way," or an unsolicited "suggestion," we go deaf. Because we know that the person speaking it does not have benevolent intentions. They are "shoulding on" us as a reflection of their own issues, their discomfort with where they are at, their challenges with embracing reality in all its forms. They need to fix us, before they can accept us. And that's the problem, right there. Acceptance opens the door to change.

Some relationships are structurally unsound. They have a kind of fragility to them, that does not lend itself to healthy functioning or relational solidity. When the trigger-winds blow, they crash to the earth, unable to sustain themselves under strain. Sometimes you can identify the primal cracks and get to work rebuilding the foundation ... but sometimes you can't. Sometimes they are too hard to see, or to feel, or to fix, and there is no way forward. This is not anyone's fault. Some relationships simply don't have the alchemy of longevity at their roots. They are here for a bit, and then they are gone. The trick is not to pretend that they were something they weren't. They may have been a great love, but love isn't a self-fulfilling prophecy. It needs a rock-solid foundation to see it through.

Beware the destroyers. They come in many forms, seldom obvious. They have given up on manifesting an actualized life, so they make it their business to undermine yours. They love empaths, and anyone with an open heart. And they prey on those who confuse actuality with potentiality. Just because you overcame the odds, doesn't mean everyone will. The closer you get to wholeness, the more important it is to be careful with who you let in. Because the destroyers can smell accomplishment from a thousand miles away. And they want to eat it… whole.

If there is one thing that distinguishes those who are able to move on from toxic families, from those who remain dysfunctionally trapped within them, it is that the former were able to disidentify with where they came from and seek their identity elsewhere. At some point, they made the courageous, bold decision that they were not them, and that they had to look elsewhere for direction and family. This is often a very difficult thing to do, because toxic families don't usually give us the love that grows us capable of taking flight, but it is the only possibility if you wish to break the cycle. Someone has to step out, and craft a new path home. Some realities are worth running from….

I have been exploring something we might call a "hurt mentality" in the last years. An unexpected event catapulted me into a painful place. And I got to experience, firsthand, the various ways that people in our society shame and shun victimhood: "Did this really happen?", "Can't you just let it go?", "No way they would have done that!", "Let's focus on the positive." It was quite a humbling experience, one that reminded me of why I have worked so hard to support others in their healing. And one where I got to see precisely why these denial mechanisms don't serve us. Because when I tried to put it away, to just let it go, to trivialize its significance, it just got worse. The truth of the experience dug in its heels, demanding to be seen, felt, spoken. Only when I brought it back into view, did it release me from its primal grip. The thing about victimhood is that it is often true. And the way beyond it is not to pretend it isn't there. It's to invite it real close, so close that it can whisper what it needs. So close that it can't help but soften its edges over time.

Pierce the smokescreen of fearful indifference.
Adventure heartily. Have faith in the shaping
of what you cannot see.

Truth is not just a concept. It's a felt experience, with embodied consequences. When we live a lie, our bones know. So do our tissues, our cells, our organs. It takes a considerable amount of energy to uphold a fake life. It debilitates us and makes us prone to disease. By contrast, we receive an enormous surge of energy when we finally live our truth. The body breathes a deep sigh of relief, delighted that it no longer has to carry the weight of the lie. It begins to move more fluidly, and to gravitate toward experiences that nourish it. So, the next time you decide to postpone making a bold leap into a more truthful life, think again. Truth is the elixir for what ails you. Truth is what you're made of.

You must never lose faith in your brilliance, no matter what the world sends your way. Your unique soul-scriptures live at the heart of you, lying in wait for their opportunity to be humanifest. They may be covered in dust, they may be hidden from view, but they are still in there, sparkling with infinite possibility.

You have to seize your path by the horns, and steer it in the direction you want. The universe won't do it for you. Nor will your friends or family. Only you can seize your day. Far too many of us are waiting for the path to do the work for us. It doesn't work like that. Your path isn't a bus that's coming to pick you up. You are your path. Don't sit around waiting for it to come to you. Get in the driver's seat and drive yourself home.

Your lack of readiness is an illusion communicated by shame-ridden parts of you that will forever have you believing that you must take a few more steps until your real life begins. It's an illusion of epic proportions. Get to it, brilliant being. There is no need to procrastinate the gateway to wholeness—it stands before you with your name on it. The world is ready for what you have to offer. No time like the presence.

LONGER
HUMANIFESTATIONS

When we have been in a state of overcoming for much of our lives, it can be difficult to surrender to the fact that there is no longer anything to overcome. Willful overcoming and goal-centeredness become an entrenched way of being—one that is associated with our very survival—and it can be difficult to slow down and realize that we made it out. That we are no longer at risk. That we created a healthier, safer reality. This is as true for people who overcame poverty as it is those who made it out of unsafe home environments. Many of us—and I am one of them—have great difficulty recognizing and integrating the fact that we are no longer back there. Our minds know we got out, but our animal bodies are still carrying the same anxieties that fueled our overcoming. In my own experience, the key to the shift in awareness is developing our capacity for surrender to our bodies. Only when we can drop down below our willful warrior, only when we can slow down and truly FEEL the change, will we be able to integrate the fact that we are no longer back there. For us to know the war is over, we have to allow ourselves to breathe deeply into the beautiful world that we have created with our own efforts. We have to raise the white flag in our hearts. This is no easy feat—surrendering brings up the old anxieties at first—but if we stay with it, it will become a natural way of being. And the wars of overcoming, slowly a thing of the past...

We don't need your faux forgiveness. We don't need your bypass-ana meditations. We don't need your perfected asanas. We don't need your detachment practices. We don't need your fake spiritual names. We don't need your victim bashing. We don't need your love and light. We don't need your law of attraction. We don't need your wishful thinking. We don't need your feeble affirmations. We don't need your perpetual positivity. We don't need your pseudo-transcendence. We don't need your flight from feeling. We don't need your claims of illusion. We don't need your stillness and silence. We don't need your patriarchal rituals and lineage. We don't need your enbullshitment enlightenment.

What we need is for you to come down from your world-avoidant perch and take all that energy you have been selfishly hoarding and give it back to humanity. What we need is for you to exit your cave of cowardice, put your tender tootsies on the ground, and actually do something to heal our species. What we need is for you to help us shape a new lineage—one that is rooted in a truly inclusive consciousness. Not a non-duality that omits everything human from the field, but one that includes all that we are, and all of our fellow humans, in its unified fold. What we need is for you to understand that ALL OF THIS is real. And that any spirituality that is bereft of humanness is a collective death knell. You want to wake up for real? Stop hiding behind your egoic badge of egolessness, and help us to heal this bloodied species.

You must tell your story. All of it, in intricate detail. You must tell it, even if there are some who are determined to stop you. Because burying your story buries your life-force. It prohibits you from actualizing all that you are meant to be. And it grants the powers-that-be control over the human narrative. We see them everywhere now, eager to censor the human voice for their own malevolent purposes. If they have their way, we will all bow in silence before them, grateful for the tyrant who has come to save us. Of course, (s)he has no interest in saving us. (S)he is entirely self-serving, seeking control for financial, egoic, psychological reasons.

So many who long for power are over-compensating for the emptiness within them. They long to feel loved by the masses, because they weren't loved as children. They long for control, so they can shield themselves from the inevitability of relational suffering. But they have come to the wrong place. Power isn't going to help them. Therapy is.

And for those of us who have been victimized by them, we find our healing in the telling of our story. We speak our truth aloud, and regain our personal sovereignty. We are at a tipping point as a collective. The repressors are picking up steam. And so are we. There is only one way to stand them down. TELL YOUR STORY. Tell it all. Tell it true.

Sometimes the growthful step is to walk further into a triggering love relationship. Sometimes the growthful step is to walk away. Every difficult love relationship is an opportunity for transformation. But that doesn't mean you have to stay. Sometimes the learning is in the leaving, the realizing that you are not where you belong, the recognition that you no longer have the energy for a labor-intensive woundmate dynamic. There is a tendency—in some psychotherapeutic circles—to assume that triggers mean that there is work to be done within the connection. Sometimes this is absolutely true. Other times, the degree of triggering is an indication that the dynamic doesn't work. That the real work 'to be done' is to finally accept that this kind of relationship is impossible, or not in your best interest. After all, a relationship is not meant to be an endurance test.

We often see this in connections where there are parental projections being lived out. Sometimes, we can do a lot of work in the heart of those primal patterns. We can heal some of our inner child dynamics and find peace with our past. But sometimes the healing comes from accepting that those dynamics don't work. They're not functional or life-enhancing. They no longer serve us. And that it's time to stop repeating the pattern and looking for love where it can't be found. Sometimes the growthful step is toward a new kind of love—one that actually meets you in your healthier places.

Individuals seldom grow at the same pace when they are coupled. One, or both partners invariably grow in different directions. Interests and priorities change, consciousness expands or contracts, one party develops while the other remains stagnant. Sometimes the relationship container is flexible enough to accommodate these differences, but not always. Sometimes it is not healthy or additive to remain together. Sometimes there is a strong impulse to say farewell. We see this often in the spiritual world. As one individual begins to awaken to their authenticity, the other remains affixed to their survivalist patterns, clinging resolutely to their adaptations and disguises, utterly refusing to expand their habitual range of e-motion. For whatever reason, they are simply not interested in exploring another way of being. And maybe for good reason. In this situation, it may seem logical that the connection must end, and this is often what happens.

But a word of caution for those who are at the beginning stages of awakening—take your time with this. In the early fires of waking up, you may feel a strong impulse to push everything away that reflects your previous self. This is natural, as you seek to deepen into a new way of being. But, do remember that once you have consolidated your awakening, you may see your partner through a different light. You may come to realize that the exact characteristics that you now see as unawakened—for example, their practicality, cynicism, and adherence to worldly matters—are precisely the qualities that ground your flight into other realms. You may come to find that their seemingly slow-to-change aspects are actually the perfect commonsense counter-balance to your rapid-fire awakening. They may be exactly what you need, in ways you were unable to recognize when your awakening caught fire. Someone had to hold down the fort while you went off in search of nirvana. The earth to your sky. Where soulmate meets solemate on the highways of transformation.

⁓

There are those who dare to suggest that trauma-survivors are too attached to their trauma. That they are perpetuating their victimhood. That they are choosing to remain stuck. Easy for them to say— they either didn't experience the same trauma, or they have worked through some of their own, or they are in complete denial. It's been my experience that those who are most affixed to the argument that we 'choose' our traumas, are usually the ones who are dissociating from theirs. Their adherence to dissociative New Cage beliefs about choice and victimhood are a dead giveaway.

Let's be clear about what we are talking about. Trauma is an embodied experience. It lives in people's bones, veins, arteries, tissues, muscles, organs. It's etched in their cells, brain, heart, and soul. Yes, it is often possible to heal our trauma-body, but not always. Not in a culture that buries trauma and that has few methodologies for deep healing. Not in a world that is still actively victimizing.

Rather than making the assumption that trauma survivors are perpetuating their victimhood, let's do something different. Let's hear their stories with a compassionate heart. Let's listen. Perhaps if we listen close enough, we will also begin to hear our own unresolved wounds rising to the surface, ready to be healed.

∾

If you grew up in a hurtful home, you may have a hard time imagining that the world can be a soft place to land. You might figure that if your family didn't hold you in high regard, no one else will. And, perhaps as a result, you hold yourself back from jumping into life, and seizing the day. Perhaps you keep yourself small and compact, skirting the edges of society, trying to go unnoticed. Perhaps you don't allow yourself to dream, because you are certain that dreams don't come true. Just like they didn't come true in your family home, where things never seemed to improve.

If this is you, I have something to tell you: It's not true. It makes perfect sense that you would feel this way, but it's just a projected expectation from your lived experience. It's all you know. But it's not all that you can know. Because there is a bounty of good people who are willing to support your efforts to create a better life. I know, because I have met many. I entered my twenties certain that the world had to be harsher than my harsh upbringing. And I was proven wrong, time and time again. Sure, there were many who were perpetuating their own ancestral toxicity, but there were also hundreds of wonderful souls, none of whom were remotely interested in abusing or scapegoating me. In fact, many of them were just like me: trauma survivors with hearts of gold, seeking safe and supportive connection. Because at heart, we are all roaming the plains looking for a loving and functional family.

It's astonishing when you realize that much of the world is kinder than your childhood home. When you do, everything starts to change. You realize that the worst is over ('worst things first'), and that you are finally free to... live.

～

Not everyone will heal in this lifetime. It's important that we accept and understand this. The perpetual emphasis on acknowledging and healing trauma is a beautiful thing, but it's not for everyone. Because some of us don't have the capacity to heal. Some can't even get out of bed, because of the weight of their pain and the complexity of their trauma. Too much has happened, and there is no possibility of transformation. This is very hard to accept in our toxic positivity culture, one where trauma is the new buzz word, and where people forget that they are not walking in someone else's shoes. Just because you were able to heal parts of your past, doesn't mean everyone can heal parts of theirs. We have all lived in a trauma-inducing culture. Some of us didn't make it through in one piece. That's a fact. And if we can just accept this, and honor and comfort them as they are without any effort to 'heal' them, we actually stand a chance of co-creating the kind of trauma-sensitive world that avoids this level of suffering altogether. Because trauma is perpetuated by insensitivity. Our tendency to turn a blind eye to the truth of people's suffering, to shame them for not healing, to blame it on their karma and their choices, is precisely the dissociative consciousness that perpetuates the trauma cycle. Better to accept people right where they are. Better to provide comfort to the fallen ones. That alone will heal the world.

It has been my experience that perhaps the most significant challenge we face as victims of narcissistic abuse is the very confusing belief that we are responsible for all of the dysfunction that existed or still exists in the connection. It is utterly essential, in order for the narcissist to benefit from the relational transaction in the way that they need to, that we believe that we are to blame for everything difficult in the relationship, and often in their lives—and it is us alone who must fix it. This misplaced sense of accountability would not work on just anyone. It worked on us, for all kinds of different reasons, one of them being that victims of narcissistic abuse tend to be responsible people readily inclined to own their role in things. And, of course, that sense of responsibility is blatantly WRONG in that context. You are not to blame for any of it, even if you currently believe that your issues attracted you to them, or that your issues contributed to your remaining connected to them.

Because that which exists in the narcissist, existed before you, and no doubt will exist beyond you. However it happened to them, however these patterns of abuse became their way of being, was a function of their own experiences, and took root independent of your presence. It is not about you now, and it was never about you. I appreciate that you may not be ready to know that yet, but I want to say this right now, as the lighthouse of understanding that you are walking towards. You may have wanted to believe that it was about you, perhaps because it gave you a sense of control—the idea that if it's your fault, then you can actually make it better. But it was NEVER ABOUT YOU. The gaslighting was not about you. The triangulation was not about you. The blaming was not about you. The playing the victim was not about you. The diminishment was not about you. The lack of empathy was never about you. The manipulation, the sense of entitlement, the ego-feeding, were never about you. They were directed AT you, but they were never about you. All of it was about them and their fragile, underdeveloped egoic structure. And there was NOT A THING you could do to change any of it.

In fact, it was strategically designed as an intrinsically unchangeable parasitic structure, one that is not seeking transformation, but is merely to be fed and maintained precisely as it is. Your job, whether you knew it or didn't know it, was to give it what it needed to maintain its current form. Devoid of the capacity for self-reflection or empathic interface, it has no fuel, no impetus to grow. And none of this is, or ever could be, your fault. They arrived in your life that way. They may have wanted you to believe it was your fault, so you would keep elevating and nourishing them. But none of that was true. None of it.

PATRIARCHAL SPIRITUALITY

Patriarchal Spirituality: Those ungrounded and inhumane "spiritual" models that have been fostered by emotionally armored, self-avoidant men.

These models share some or all of the following beliefs:

- The ego is the enemy of a spiritual life
- The "monkey mind" is the cause of suffering
- Your feelings are an illusion
- Your personal identifications and stories are necessarily false
- Witnessing your pain transforms it
- Your body is a spiritually bankrupt toxic quagmire
- The only real consciousness is an "absolute" and "transcendent" one
- Stillness and silence are THE path
- Isolation is the best way to access "higher states"
- There is no "self"
- Meditation is THE royal road to enlightenment

- Enlightenment actually exists
- Formlessness is superior to form
- The ultimate path is upward and vertical
- Real spirituality exists independent of our humanness

In fact, most of the above is a blatant lie. Here are more accurate hypotheses about the nature of human life:

- A healthy ego is beautifully essential to healthy functioning
- The monkey mind is a reflection of the monkey heart (the unresolved emotional body)
- Many of our identities and stories are fundamental to who we are, where we have been, why we are here
- Healing our pain transforms it; watching it is only a preliminary step
- Our bodies are our spiritual temples
- The only "real" consciousness is one that integrates all that we are and all that this life is
- Stillness and silence are only one path; many people prefer movement, sound, and expression

- There is no "higher" state (we aren't birds). But inter-personal connection may be the best way to access deepened states

- There is a magnificent self; the work is to align it with your sacred purpose, not to deny it altogether

- Meditation is not THE royal road; it's one road, and it is not any more effective than embodied movement and emotional release as clarification and transformation tools

- Enlightenment does not exist; Enrealment does. (Be real now.) And it's a relative experience, changing form as our self and our life changes form

- We are glorious form, and we are here to in-form our humanness

- If there is an "ultimate path," it's downward, rooted, and horizontal

- There is no distinction between our spirituality and our humanness

The wool has been pulled over our eyes. Men who were too unhealthily egoic to admit that they couldn't deal with their humanness, their feelings, their traumas, had to find a system that smoke-screened their avoidance. They found it. It's called "Enlightenment." It's also called "Spiritual Mastery." And it usually involves leaving the world, in one form or another. This way, they can convince themselves and others that they have mastered the one true path.

In fact, Enlightenment is just a construct that is designed to avoid the multi-faceted nature of reality. In fact, they are mastering nothing. They are merely fleeing their fragmentation, their confusion, and the fact that they don't know how to find their center in the heart of the world. Don't be fooled. They know less about reality than day-to-day people. They know less about reality than those who live from their hearts. They are camouflaging their unresolved trauma beneath a 'realization mask.'

What we need now are models that lead us back into our hearts, into relatedness, into a deep and reverential regard for the self. Those models may invite us to detach temporarily in an effort to see ourselves through a different lens, but they will not leave us out there, floating into the eternal emptiness and calling that a life.

Detachment is a tool—it's NOT a life.

The models we need will then invite us back into our bodies, back into our feelings, back into connection with our marvelous planet and with each other. No more "enlightened" masters sitting in caves while the women of the village bring them food. If you can't find your transformation in the village, you haven't found shit. The new models will invite us to integrate what we find "out there" with who we are "in here." They will invite us to embody the now, rather than to pretend we have found it in the heart of our dissociation.

It's time to co-create spiritual models that begin, and end, within our wondrous humanness.

It's not "out there," dear friends. It's right here, inside these aging body temples.

To arrive at this place in my life, I had to overcome so very much. I had to overcome emotionally unwell parents, crippling abandonment issues, childhood poverty, internalized shame and self-doubt. I had to punch my way through endless challenges as I worked to become a lawyer, to let go of law, to surrender to writing as a path. I had to knock on hundreds of thousands of doors in frigid Canadian winters to sell windows so I could afford to write through the night. I had to fight for my right to the light, time and time again, for more than five decades.

When people ask me how and why I did it, I only have one answer—Soul. Not masochism, not the need to be acknowledged but, instead, the deep need to fully excavate and actualize my soul's voice—my reasons for being, my entelechy, my sacred purpose. I was driven by a desperate longing to be who I was called to become in this lifetime. And as difficult as it was to find and live that voice, it was easier than the uncomfortable alternative. It was easier than living a lie.

Wherever you find yourself on your journey through time, be assured that there is a soul path somewhere at the heart of it. And, as difficult as it may be to see it, as overwhelming as it may seem to embody it, it is well worth the effort. Once you catch a glimpse of it, it will beckon you home, like a fire of divine possibility with your name on it. And that fire will not only show you the direction to walk, it will fuel you as you overcome the obstacles in the way. It will warm and inspire your every step.

When you walk through the gateway of your sacred purpose, you walk into yourself. Blessingly buffered from the madness of the world, your purpose filters out those relationships and energies that undermine your expansion. Infused with vitality and a clarified focus, new pathways of possibility appear where before there were obstacles. Life still has its challenges, but you interface with them differently, coated in an authenticity of purpose that sees through the veils to what really matters.

Don't lose the faith, wherever you are on the path. Keep going...

About the Author

Jeff Brown is a breakthrough voice in the self-help/ spirituality field, and the author of seven popular books: *Soulshaping: A Journey of Self-Creation, Ascending with Both Feet on the Ground, Love It Forward, An Uncommon Bond, Spiritual Graffiti, Grounded Spirituality,* and *Hearticulations.*

In his previous life, Jeff was a criminal lawyer and psychotherapist. Since pursuing his path as a writer, he has launched many initiatives, including founding Enrealment Press, and an online school, Soulshaping Institute. He is the producer and key journeyer of the award-winning spiritual documentary, Karmageddon, which also stars Ram Dass, Seane Corn, Deva Premal and Miten. He has written a series of inspirations for ABC's Good Morning America and appeared on over 300 radio shows. He also authored the viral blog 'Apologies to the Divine Feminine (from a warrior in transition).'

A popular presence in social media, Jeff's new terms and well-loved quotes became a phenomenon some years ago, and continue to be shared by millions of seekers and growers worldwide. His quotes have been shared in social media by The David Suzuki Foundation, Brain Games host Jason Silva, author Amanda De Cadenet, actress Chrissy Metz, songstress LeAnn Rimes, and many others. Most beautifully, they have touched and benefitted millions of souls.

Jeff now understands that each step on his path laid down the foundation of a new model: Grounded Spirituality. The challenges he faced, and the countless steps of overcoming were intended for this purpose: to support humanity in their efforts to embody all that they are. Not to bypass their humanness, but to celebrate it. Not to find enlightenment independent of the self, but to find enrealment deep within it. Here we are, just as we are.

Jeff currently lives in Canada with his wife, poet Susan Frybort. He is presently breaking new ground as an Enrealment Activist, having just launched

The Enrealment Hour Podcast and The Enrealment Newsletter (https://jeffbrown42.substack.com/). In addition, he is hard at work on four new books and courses, and looking forward to whatever other unexpected surprises await this wildly rich path of Sacred Purpose.

You can connect with his offerings at jeffbrown.co, soulshapinginstitute.com, karmageddonthemovie.com, and enrealment.com. He is grateful for your presence and for your support.